THE OUTER CIRCLE

THE OUTER CIRCLE

RAMBLES IN REMOTE LONDON

BY

THOMAS BURKE

LONDON : GEORGE ALLEN & UNWIN LTD.
RUSKIN HOUSE, 40 MUSEUM STREET W.C. 1

First published in 1921

TO

WINIFRED

SUBURBIA

Where London sprawls across the gentle fields,
In those far fringes where the green begins—
Eltham and Enfield, Southall and Wanstead Flat—
The landscape but a loveless prospect yields ;
Wan grass, the last week's washing, a dead cat,
Factories, maisonettes and sardine-tins.

Yet even here the honeysuckle blows,
And the shy nightingale enchants the gloom ;
And sometimes I have seen the wild white rose
Around the hawthorn bough at Barnet Fair ;
And when the evening flowers with lights of home,
Each window seems a little silent prayer.

CONTENTS

THE OUTER CIRCLE

SETTING OUT

THE shameful accident happened during Armistice Week. I was lost in London. I, whose virgin ears suffered their earliest wooing from the bells of St. Mary-le-Bow, lost myself in London.

On the second evening of that week, when the excitement had over-reached itself to an anti-climax, I boarded a motor 'bus. Its head-board was obscured by a festoon of legs and skirts of joy-riding armisticers, but I was careless of its destination. London had capitulated to alien revellers, and I was glad to join the refugees and escape towards the suburbs.

For the first twenty minutes I checked our route : Oxford Street, Marble Arch, Praed Street, Maida Vale, Kilburn, " The Crown," Cricklewood, Shoot-up Hill. Then a sudden lurch brought four soldiers and three girls against my tender spot, and I went to the floor, and, for the space of many minutes, saw nothing of London. After much battling, the black legs and khaki legs were withdrawn by their owners, and I was extricated. Then, across the new-

lit night broke a cry, " All Change.   Garage only ! "
With the others I slung myself over the front of the
'bus and dropped to the roadway.

"Where are we ? " I cried to the glooms.   And
the glooms gave back : " Sherrick Green."   " Sherrick Green," I mused.   " Sherrick Green.   Now
where in Middlesex or Hertfordshire is that ?   And is
it on the Great Central, the Northern, the Midland
or on the North-Western ?   And how the devil am
I to get back to town ? "

How far we had travelled during the minutes
that I lay prone I could not judge.   My companions
of the journey had suddenly melted into the darkness, and with them the 'bus ; but a few yards
distant some shrouded lights hinted at humanity.
They seemed to hang in the middle air.   They
illuminated nothing of their surroundings, and threw
no beam.   Like respectable citizens, they kept
themselves *to* themselves.   I approached them, and
found that they were attached to a small shop
wherein sweets, tobacco, toys and newspapers were
hidden.   I entered, bought a newspaper and some
cigarettes, and inquired for a back number of Sexton
Blake.   While the good woman foraged for it I
made talk.

" Nice part round here—Sherrick Green.   Haven't
been this way before."

" Yes," she replied from the lower recesses of the
counter.

" Nice little houses you've got here. Easy reach
of London, too. So convenient, and all that."

" London ? You talk as though we was miles
in the country. . . . I got the week before last's, but
that ain't the one, is it ? "

" Oh, when I said London, I was thinking of
Charing Cross."

" Oh, Charing Cross, yes. . . . Ah, 'ere we are.
. . . ' The House Behind the Willows.' That's it,
ain't it ? "

" Thanks, yes. That's the one I missed. . . . Er—
if I keep straight on here, it won't take ten minutes
to—er——" I struck a match and lit a cigarette,
and in the pause the information that I sought for
came pat.

" No, about ten minutes to Willesden. Straight
on."

I fled. Ten minutes to Willesden. I was in
London, then—at Sherrick Green, N.W. I stood
on the deserted pavement and burned with shame.
Sherrick Green, London ; and I had never heard of
it ! A corner of my own city, where men ate and
slept, and loved and hated ; where tradesmen built
bonny businesses ; where babies were born ; where
children went to school and grew into men and
women ; and I knew not of it. Other remote
suburbs I knew and loved. I had seen the lilac
bushes exterminated from Crofton Park. I was
about when the tramway was extended from Tooting

to Hampton Court. I had watched the steady surge of houses from Lewisham to Sidcup. I had witnessed Croydon's absorption of Addiscombe. I had seen Elthorne and Charlton brought into the London Postal District, and Rippleside and Chingford brought within a 'bus ride of Victoria. Yet Sherrick Green I had cut.

I felt that I owed it amends, so I humbly moved about its streets until I came to the domain of its parent, Neasden. Walking thus, I had the sense of visiting the city of a strange country. In Cheapside, in Fleet Street, Lothbury and Holborn I must at some time or other have rubbed shoulders with Sherrick Greeners, and have seen them as other men who lived with me at Highgate. Yet here, in their own territory, I saw them savagely themselves, insular, prejudiced against the natives of other countries who walked with them the streets of the inner city.

I wondered how far my ignorance was shared by other men not Sherrick Greeners. I remembered many place-names, casually dismissed by those who did not live there as " dormitories of London "—Fortis Green, Bowes Park, Stroud Green, Whetstone, Harringay, Rushey Green, Ponder's End, Cyprus ; and then and there I decided that these little towns must be celebrated. I would lock up ; gather toothbrush, comb and razor, and re-visit them ; make the Grand Tour of the true heart of London. I would

see again these sweet-named Parks and Greens
whose air is fed by the dreams of youth and man;
these scorned dormitories where high schemes are
laid, and where ambitions and aspirations of men
and women slumber in the seed until they are
brought to flower in the huckster-place of E.C.
or W.

Back in town I called at the Club, where other
armisticers were gathered.

" Hullo, old chap. Where've you been ? "

" I've been to Sherrick Green," I replied, self-
consciously, as one might say " I am this moment
from Illyria."

" Sherrick Green ? Oh, in the country. You've
missed all the excitement then."

" Do you mean to say," I demanded solemnly,
" that you've lived all these years in London and
don't know Sherrick Green ? "

" Never heard of the place. Not ashamed to own
it, either. If Sherrick Green were worth knowing,
I should have heard of it. Where is it ? "

" It's in London. Near Willesden."

" Oh, one of those new suburbs that used to be
built overnight, I suppose."

" It is," I replied. " It is one of those new suburbs
on old acres. And therefore it is a place that every
good Londoner, and every student of the human
heart, should visit. You go and stare at some crumbling pile made by some predatory prelate some

five hundred years ago, and from your rubber-necking you offer yourself some manufactured thrill. It's all wrong The true thrill should come when you look at the new suburb and its half-built roads and houses, and remember that Mr. Wilkinson has taken that little house which still wants windows and is not yet connected to main drainage, and is waiting to take his bride into it; that there they will begin their married life, and there will the young Wilkinsons be born. We know the history of your worm-eaten Gothic piles. Their tale is told; their course finished. Men have done with them. But the potentialities of the history of that red-brick villa in that clay-soil suburb are too vast for contemplation. To ignore such places as these is to mark yourself Philistine. Yes, Philistine to you, sir. Good-night."

Elsewhere I found equal ignorance of those suburbs to which trams, 'buses and trains go in their hundreds all the day. It was clear that the only people who knew them were 'bus drivers and the people who lived there. A few had heard of Ladywell, Harlesden, Brockley Tips, Parson's Green; but none had seen them, save one man who lived at Brockley and who exceeded myself in disgust and indignation at their insular ignorance. And when I asked him if he had ever been to Cyprus he said he could't afford these Mediterranean trips. When I told him that hundreds of people crossed the Thames

every night to their homes in Cyprus he was face-
tiously incredulous.

Motor 'buses carry these place-names to all parts
of London, and men pass through their railway
stations on the way out of London. But little of
their shape or character is heeded ; random flashes
of trim gardens and a steady flood of roofs are all
that the traveller sees. The stations are seldom
busy. It is not now fashionable for suburbs to
have railway stations. Have you not seen the
derelict stations of the inner suburbs—poor, towzled
affairs, lonely as wayside halts, but grimy, snivelly,
tatterdemalion brothers of the open-air halt ? All
trains seem to have forgotten them. Sometimes
you see the staff—or a portion of it—purposeless
officials, mooning about the vast platforms. These
take their tone from the station. Staff, fittings,
appointments, the very advertisement posters, are
flat and woolly. There stand these stations—
Wandsworth Road, Coborn Road, Globe Road,
Cambridge Heath, London Fields, Walworth Road,
Queen's Road, Borough Road, Camberwell Road,
Elephant and Castle, Loudoun Road, Queen's Park,
Haggerston, Gospel Oak, Spa Road, Tidal Basin,
Leman Street, Blackhorse Road, Barnsbury, Canon-
bury, Haydon's Road, Royal Oak, Woodgrange Park,
and the station that is, without prefix, named Park—
there they stand, frayed and forlorn, above or below
the main current of London traffic, out of the public

ken ; the world forgetting, by the world forgot.
And the stations of the outer suburbs are in little
better case, save that excitement does visit them
between seven and ten in the morning and between
six and eight in the evening, when their natives go
forth and return.

Seldom does a stray tourist alight at Palmer's
Green, or Cranley Gardens, or Maryland Point as the
beginning of a walking tour.   Even those who make
a point of boring you with tediously dilated stories
of the shrines of central London and of the " places
of interest " within a four-mile radius, ignore the
hundred venerable relics of the suburbs.   Hampton
Court they know, and Richmond Palace and Eltham
Palace.   But they never conduct parties to Anne
Boleyn's house, to Eastbury Manor, to Battersea
Rise House, to Morden College, to the Bishop of
Rochester's House or Bruce Castle.   They would
consider it time ill-spent to ponder upon the trim
roads of Thornton Heath or the nervous streets
of Upton Park.   They are of those who conceive a
suburb as a Euclidian arrangement of villas, each
bearing to its dull neighbour the equality of the
angle at A to that at B, or the resemblance of one
soldier on parade to another.   To the uninformed eye
a regiment of soldiers shows uniformity, nothing
more.   But behind each tunic is a passionate personality ; the angle at A is bursting with suppressed
A-ness.   I have never yet in my wanderings met a

truly dull man in the suburbs. From the most
amorphous material bits of bright life will break out,
if the sympathetic agent be employed. Plain men
will twitch a curtain and discover to you a hall of
wonder whose existence they themselves have well-
nigh, but not wholly, smothered. I have had great
joy of borough councillors in Harringay ; have met
kindred minds in ironmongers at Bowes Park ;
policemen of Rushey Green have discoursed to me on
the beauty of the dawn, as it comes up like thunder
from the flats of Kent ; and a bookmaker of Finchley
has rejoiced me by an admiration of James Sant's
Soul's Awakening. Browning wanted " to know a
butcher paints ": I have met one who does. I
met a journeyman baker who wished to discuss the
atomic theory ; and I once knew a landlord at
Highgate who wanted to accompany Shackleton on
his last voyage. Dull men I have met in Pall Mall
clubs, and in literary and art centres; but a dull
shop-keeper with a one-man business in the suburbs
is rare.

But I was speaking of the deplorable lack of
communication between suburbs. A Manchester man
is just a Manchester man. But the Londoner from
Kilburn is a Kilburn man, who smiles wanly when
you speak of Walthamstow. He does not hate the
Walthamstowite as the Yorkshireman hates the
Lancashire lad. He just ignores him. London is
no longer a city ; it is an assembly of camps, whose

members ask nothing of their neighbours. Stroud
Green knows nothing of the ways and thoughts of
Elegant Eltham, and cares less. East Sheen is deaf
to the wailings of Clissold Park. Crime in one camp
may draw the languid attention of camps far removed,
but nothing short of this can awaken interest.

Men of London will buy and read the *Manchester
Guardian*, the *Birmingham Post* and the *Glasgow
Herald*, but I never heard of a Whetstonian who read
the *Sidcup Times* or a Raynes Parker who " took in "
the *Hornsey Journal*. To these suburban organs is
given the facetious contempt that is given to the
suburb itself; yet, through them, the music of
humanity surges more fully than through any metropolitan organ pre-occupied with the universal. The
latter tells you only of the death of a Duchess,
of a speech by Lloyd George, of the marriage of a
prince: events that arouse neither pity nor terror;
but these more definite sheets have tales for you to
move the heart to those emotions that at once ennoble
and abase us. As for him who says that his local
paper occupies itself with recording the trivial, I
have no patience with him. Awkward adolescent
towns the suburbs may be, but' they are mighty
precocious adolescents. I take at random the current
issue of the voice of my own northern suburb.
Listen :

*Presentation to Mr. Yapp; Forty Years' Service at the
Works. . . . Pretty Wedding at St. Andrew's. . . . Child*

Falls from Window. . . . Councillor Hinks on Trashy Books in the Public Library. . . . Threatened Rise in Rates ; Spirited Protest by Councillor Brighteye. . . . Runaway Horse in the High Road ; Widow's Stall Wrecked. . . . Mr. Simp's Lecture on Lake Lucerne.

Trivial, says my gentleman ! Why, the whole paper throbs. It is alive. Turn to the back page, to the advertisement columns. Here again is the beat of life ; very insistent in that column which the editor crudely heads " For Sale and Exchange," and which I have named " All Souls' Parade." Through that column Peeping Toms may watch the procession of the souls of their borough, fluttering under their gauze of anonymity. All the lofty ambitions and the grievous woes of our streets are adumbrated here, and the contemplative may brood upon the solid body of anguish or delight that lies hehind. Thus, what accumulation of unfruitful endeavour, precipitating him to despair, led Box 340 to insert the following heart-cry at a cost of two shillings and sixpence :

" Cockerel, three pullets, two laying hens. Would exchange for gramophone records."

It is followed by an appeal that makes uncomfortable suggestions to the imagination :

" Wanted coffee stall, portable clothes copper (10 gall.) and kitchen table."

Happier in tone is the next. One sees the whilom invalid arising from his suburban couch and trotting

to his back-garden, ready to throw a match with
Adam in the primal pastime of man :

> " Recipe for home-made remedy for indigestion. Adver-
> tiser cured himself. Would exchange for gardening imple-
> ments."

A curious application follows from an individual
who seems cursed with hesitation in great moments :

> " Allotment half required. Would share tools and seeds."

It would seem idle to reply to that advertisement.
By the time the word reaches him he may have made
up his mind that he does not want an allotment.
At present he only half-requires it, and may be waiting for a sign to drive him one way or the other.
Or has the printer made a slip ? Perhaps, adopting
the colloquial manner that seems to be the present
fashion in advertising, he really wrote " Allotment
not 'arf required " in a spirit of flagrant enthusiasm.
This is one of the hundred enigmas that confront
you on All Souls' Parade.

Surely those idle minds that seriously debate
the question " Are the Suburbs Soulless ? " cannot
have read their local papers. I have great delight
of local papers. Tastes in bedside books are as
sharply varied as tastes in tobaccos and perfumes.
For the half-hour before sleep some choose the
exuberance of the detective story ; some the shifting
emotions of the picaresque novel ; others, the warm

serenity of Montaigne, Lamb or Burton. But for me the chief shepherd of dreams is the local newspaper ; and at my bedside I keep a body of these lords of pretty pastures. Wherever I go about London and about England, I never return without the current issue of the local journal. You should see my collection. It includes copies of the *Westmoreland Gazette*, the *Southport Visitor*, the *Wood Green Sentinel*, the *Tottenham Herald*, the *Islington Daily Gazette*, the *Clapham Observer*, the *Brixton Free Press*, the *Hornsey Journal*, the *Hampstead and Highgate Express*, the *Finchley Press*, the *Eltham Times*, the *East Ham Echo*, the *Barnet Chronicle*, the *Staffordshire Sentinel*, the *Huddersfield Examiner*, the *Burnley News*, the *East Anglian Times*, the *Scarborough Post*, the *Bath Herald*, the *Glasgow Bulletin*, the *Bradford Telegraph*, the *Clifton Chronicle*.

If only these journals had a wider range of "exchanges," there would be born a rapprochement between suburbs, and the North's indifference to the South, and the West's to the East would be no more. A little understanding between suburbs, as between nations, would breed sympathy and respect and, later, keen interest. It is as an attempt to introduce the far suburbs one to another that I present this book. "The Outer Circle" which I have followed is that which marks the eight-mile radius from St. Paul's ; and many goodly places are to be found upon its border. You may have as goodly adventure at Parson's Green as in the Strand or alongside the Docks, and as rough excitement of mind and body in Finsbury Park as in Spitalfields or Leicester Square. Of these places I pretend to show you only form and feature ; of their inwardness I cannot talk. It is my purpose only to drive you to seek for yourselves the souls of your own and adjoining suburbs. And if you gather from your study one-tenth of the delight that has come to me in revisiting these little towns, you will be doing very well.

TOTTENHAM

" The paradise of the London worker."—Local Guide.

IF you start from Holloway and pursue Seven Sisters Road to its end you will come to Tottenham. You may exclaim : " Who on earth wants to come to Tottenham ? " Well, quite a number of people live at Tottenham, and thousands of strangers go regularly to Tottenham, not to see the parish church, or the room where Queen Elizabeth slept, but to see the game of football played at the ground of the Tottenham Hotspurs.

I first went to Tottenham one fine Saturday, when I had nothing better to do. I had not meant to go to Tottenham. A tramcar, labelled Waltham Cross, attracted me at Tottenham Court Road by its bright colour and firm lines. I boarded it. Until then my journeys along Seven Sisters Road had ceased at Finsbury Park. There seemed no just cause for going farther. At Finsbury Park was The Manor House, and at The Manor House was a large concert-room, with tables and chairs negligently scattered about it ; and there family parties would gather and order refreshment of alert waiters and listen to a string band, which afforded

fluent music. So here one rested and speculated
in security on what lay beyond of peril and mis-
chance, and possible benightment.

But that day there was no such lure. The Manor
House music-room was closed, and I suffered the
car to bear me away. I took the hazards of the
road. From Holloway to Finsbury Park Station,
Seven Sisters Road is a long line of poor shops
that have not quite made up their minds what
produce they shall stock, and elegant residences
that have come down in the world and are now
addresses for little mail-order businesses. The very
road is vacillating in character, and seems not to
know whether it should be reticent and grave, or
rude and matey. It seems to have relaxed all
effort, and to have yielded to any external influence
that may beat upon it. It seems almost too tired
to go anywhere; and I was astonished when I
discovered how far this wounded snake had dragged
its slow length along, shedding, on the way, some
half-hundred desultory by-streets. It has suffered
two terrible gashes; one in the tail and one near
the head. The length between is bright and whole.

You are shocked when this meagre street changes
to solid prosperity, as it does between Finsbury
Park and Amhurst Park Road; and shocked again
when the opulence crumbles to decay in its final
section; and shocked yet again when you escape
from these squalors at Seven Sisters Corner into

High Road, Tottenham ; Tottenham, which, according to Domesday Book, a Countess Judith held of
the King for five hides.

Here are the seven beautiful sister-trees that
commemorate the original seven. Here is Tottenham Green, now broken into small grassy spaces.
Here is the Broadway, with more trees, each tree
furnished with a circular seat where still the village
fathers gather at evening. " Tottenham is a bright,
cheerful, and progressive place, whether regarded
from a residential or commercial aspect." This you
may learn from the guide-book. From six months'
study of the daily newspapers you may learn, too, that
Tottenham appears in the police-courts news more
often than any other London borough. Press
and guide-book thus seem to be in agreement. Jane
Cakebread was a native of Tottenham. That old
ballad, " The Tournament of Tottenham," is not
yet out of date. Tottenham, with its centuries of
history, is young. It guards a dower of great story
and increases it.

At Tottenham, you may remember, begins and
ends the most joyous book in the English tongue.
" You are well overtaken, gentlemen ! " cries
Piscator on the opening page. ." A good morning
to you both ; I have stretched my legs up Tottenham
Hill to overtake you, hoping your business may
occasion you towards Ware, whither I am going
this fine, fresh May morning." And Venator at

the end of his five instructive days with Piscator, expresses his thanks at Tottenham High Cross in good fashion. " I will requite a part of your courtesies with a bottle of sack, milk, oranges, and sugar ; which, all put together, make a drink like nectar ; indeed, too good for any but us anglers." And over the sack he sings Sir Henry Wotton's song to Anglers. In that " sweet shady arbour," near the High Cross, Piscator speaks the last words : " Study to be quiet."

Well, we too may to-day stretch our legs up Tottenham Hill, and may overtake good companions ; and, amid the happy noise of its industrial community, we may follow the pious teaching of good Isaac as seriously as amid the " sweet shady arbours " that he found there. " The Swan," where he sometimes called for his morning draught, still opens its doors at noon ; but it can provide none of that nectar ; nor can the little fish restaurant serve you with carp as ordered by Piscator :

" Take a carp, alive if possible, scour him, and rub him clean with water and salt, but scale him not ; then, open him, and put him, with his blood and his liver, which you must save when you open him, into a small pot or kettle ; then take sweet marjoram, thyme, and parsley, of each half a handful, a sprig of rosemary, and another of savory, bind them into two or three small bundles, and put them to your carp, with four or five whole onions, twenty pickled oysters, and three anchovies. Then pour upon your carp as much claret wine as will only cover him, and season your claret well with salt, cloves, and mace, and the rinds of oranges and lemons ; that done, cover your pot and set

it on a quick fire till it be sufficiently boiled ; then take out
the carp and lay it with the broth into the dish, and pour
upon it a quarter of a pound of the best fresh butter, melted
and beaten with half-a-dozen spoonfuls of the broth, the
yolks of two or three eggs, and some of the herbs shred ;
garnish your dish with lemons, and so serve it up, and much
good do you."

But the tale of junketings and cakes and ale is
not yet fully told. Along the centuries come echoes
of the merry times that have been round the High
Cross on the Green, and the echoes are caught and
their notes repeated ; for Tottenham is a crowded
London suburb, the domain of young people.
There is a heartiness about it that comes refresh-
ingly to the visitor from Highgate, where heartiness
is forbidden. Joy persists. There are still songs
to be sung. Here are still groups of those who hear
the chimes at midnight from All Hallows', and play
their pranks beneath the minatory chimneys that
adjoin the recreation ground. Here are still girls
and gardens, and moonrise, bold ribbons, shy silks
and muslins ; and the hearts of the boys beat bravely.
" Back to her nest comes the swallow in the Spring-
time," whispers Rodolphe in *La Bohème* ; and if
you go to Tottenham at the time of the breaking
of buds, you will see in the faces of the factory boys
and girls the recurrent throb of beauty. While
Highgate's motto reads : " It *looks* so bad," the
motto of Tottenham is : " Who cares ? "

They live well at Tottenham. It is your good
fortune to find that, though " progressive," it does

not move all the way with the times. One may be happy at Tottenham. It supports a large music-hall, a dozen or so picture-palaces, the football ground, and good inns with good keepers. It owns open-air swimming-baths, a Grammar School, two public libraries, vast tracts of waters, the stately Bruce Castle in Bruce Park, and part of the River Lea. It also owns the greater length of a pleasant stream called " The Moselle," which runs, or rather crawls, from Muswell Hill, to which it gave a name, under Lordship Lane into the Lea. Surely here is enough to bring content to the keenest and most curious appetite for joy. How pleasant, for instance, to be able to date your correspondence from Tottenham-on-Moselle.

Nor is this all. There are many minor delights to be had by the voracious. In the High Road is a secondhand bookshop kept by a Mr. Fisk, who has written histories, full and clustering, of Tottenham and Edmonton. In his shop I discovered a treasure : the author's signed copy of a novel, published locally in the 'eighties :

THE OLD BULL INN OF EDMONTON

by

THOMAS LEE, plasterer

At the Old Bull Inn
Silver Street
Edmonton
1882

The publican as publisher is a new idea. I wish my publisher would turn publican, and send me my royalties in cask and bottle. This reminds me of another new idea of mine for publishers.

I have lately, like most modern authors, had the doubtful pleasure of seeing a film-version of one of my stories. I had always regarded this story as invented and told by me; and (again, like most modern authors) I was surprised when a certain skilled workman, called a producer, claimed it as his. I expressed this surprise in one or two quarters, and was told not to be silly.

Well, well——. But it does lacerate one's vanity to see this kind of thing: " D. W. Griffith's great film tragedy will shortly be seen at the —— Cinema." " In creating this tragic story, D. W. Griffith hopes to strike out a new line." " D. W. Griffith presents his poignant Limehouse drama." " Miss Mary Pickford in *her* new film, ' Soapsuds.' " And so on.

I want to know the reason for this. Perhaps it is good for the author to be knocked off his perch now and then; but is it good that pedestrian mechanics should claim what is not theirs? In the theatrical world it is the same. One sees on programmes this kind of thing: Mr. Middle Mann, in conjunction with Mr. Gus Michigan, presents Jennie Jones in his latest production, " The Man who Went Upstairs." What these people had to do with writing the play is not made clear; but

throughout the run it is described as " their " play.
The author's name must be sought among the
advertisements with a magnifying-glass.

Why should these people make this false claim
to the product of other men's brains ? By themselves they can do nothing. They can present,
but they cannot invent. They are skilled labourers,
whose relation to an author's work is similar to that
of printers, binders, and publishers. The position
of the play-actor is that of the printer ; he takes
other men's work and gives it an attractive appearance. He is a go-between, carrying the author's
written word to a larger number of people than
the author, individually, could reach. When he
assumes the title " artist," and claims to " create "
character, he is merely impudent ; as impudent as
the bricklayer who credits himself with the architect's
brains. The position of the producer, who always
speaks of *his* production, is that of the publisher.
Yet we do not find publishers calling themselves
creative artists or claiming credit for the work of
their authors. When we pick up a book we find
the author's name in good black type on title-page,
cover, and jacket, and the publisher's imprint in
modest type at the bottom of page, cover, and
jacket.

The actor and the producer have very little to do
with the success of a play. The greatest and most
popular actor of his time cannot draw an audience

to a poor play ; the most indifferent company of players can fill a theatre with a good play. But if the producer and the actor may lay claim to other people's work, then the publisher may do so.

And this is my idea : that publishers should come into line with the theatre and the " movie " world. Let them " feature " themselves. Let us have no more of this disgusting truckling to the vanity of the wretched working-man who *writes* the stuff. If you pay him for his work, what right has he to expect a place on the " bill " ? Let us hear no more of " Mr. Compton Mackenzie's new novel," or " Mr. John Masefield's great tragedy." Let us have something like this :

MESSRS. MIDDLEMEN & CO.

Present

Their Great New Work of Humour,

" THE PICKWICK PAPERS,"

Printed by Messrs. Long, Primer & Co.

Comp.-ing by Fred Jones, Arthur Brown, Harry Robinson, and Jack Smith.

Machined by Messrs. Stereo, Matrix, Mould and C'otype,

On Paper manufactured by White, Ragg & Co.,

Bound by Messrs. Straw, Bord & Co.

And, in some obscure corner (in nonpareil, please, Printer) :

Or like this :

Coming Shortly !

The Art and Crafty Press' Remarkable Life of Dr. Samuel Johnson.

Never has the A. & C covered such a wide range of human interest in one book. Here are observation, humour, sharp character-drawing, brilliant dialogue. The A. & C. has at last produced the perfect biography. The A. & C. is indebted to some slight extent to a rough manuscript by J. Boswell, and they have here shown what great artists can do with slender material.

That's the style. No doubt advertisements in this vein would arouse bitter indignation ; yet they are not a bit more arrogant or misleading than the claims of those skilled mechanics—producers, actors, and managers. I offer the idea to some enterprising young publisher. He need not fear that he will lose by it. Authors will put up with anything. They are the tamest creatures, and would feed out of a publisher's hand—if he ever gave them the chance.

Pardon this digression ; I was led into it by the blessed word " publisher." Let us get back to High Road, Tottenham. Among its minor delights, for me, was that of discovering, in a newsagent's window, some rare publications, which carried me back to the days of my youth and to the Penny Readings in the Church Schools.

Yes, in Tottenham they are still offering the poems of W. A. Eaton, each poem printed on a galley slip, price one penny, the price which I paid many years ago for my copy of " The Fireman's Wedding." Honour to his publishers for resisting the temptation to profiteer. Honour to Tottenham for thus nurturing his fame.

The unbeautiful Cross which stands midmost the tide of Tottenham's business is not that in whose shade Isaac Walton rested ; it was erected in 1889 by a local ecclesiastic to replace the old wooden cross that was then crumbling to touchwood. Since the fifteenth century a cross has stood there. " There has been a cross here of long continuance, even so long as since the decree was made by the Church that every parish should in places most frequented set up a Cross." It is not an Eleanor Cross, though it follows the form of those erected at the halting-places of that queen's remains. It was in existence before that event, and, according to an old topographist, was " re-edified and peradventure raised higher " in anticipation of the procession passing through Tottenham. Near the Cross are some gracious groups of almshouses—Reynardson's Almshouses, the Pound Almshouses, the Sanchez Almshouses, and the Sailmakers' Almshouses—and the rest of the High Road buildings fit aptly with these cottages. There are no soaring shops or many-storied houses; all are flat, and low-pitched, making no endeavour towards the grandiose. The oldest of the charities is the

Sanchez group, which were built in 1596 by a baker who baked for Philip of Spain and visited England with him. After having suffered many renovations they now stand empty, condemned as unfit for habitation.

Tottenham's other famous relic is Bruce Castle, now a public museum, mainly of zoological specimens. The present building dates from the sixteenth century, but the original castle was the property of Robert Bruce, who settled there after his vain bid for the crown of Scotland. It was rebuilt by a courtier of Henry VIII, who there received his royal master. Thereafter it passed through various hands, falling step by step from its high estate. Sir Rowland Hill purchased it early in the nineteenth century and made a boarding school of it ; and a school it remained until, in 1891, the alert local council secured castle and grounds for the public. The old parish church, bowed with years as it is, can hardly be called a relic, for very little of its original fabric remains. It suffered " restoration " in 1876. Its records are yellow, for, according to a copy of a charter to be found on its walls, King David of Scotland bestowed it in the twelfth century on the Canons of Holy Trinity, London. Among its many treasures is one of human, rather than spiritual, interest. This is to be found in the belfry —a silver-toned bell, which was the bell used as an alarm-signal to the garrison of Quebec. It was

captured at the siege of Quebec by a group of
drunken seamen who surprised its guard before a
note could be struck from it. What has Mr. Pussyfoot
to say to that ?

Next the High Road, Tottenham's most important
thoroughfare is Lordship Lane, which connects it
with Wood Green. Of Lordship Lane the local
guide says : " This fine thoroughfare. . . Walking
or riding down it, one finds it easy to imagine the
period when it was open country and pleasantly
rural in appearance." Does one ? I don't. I can
more easily find the skylark in Ludgate Hill. It
has no air of Lordship. It cringes. It seems very
sorry for itself. It meanders, rather than goes,
to Wood Green. I speak only of its physical features—its houses, shops, and waste places—not
of its people : I am sure they do not cringe. It
affects one with torpor after the bright business of
the High Road. Now there certainly is something
lordly about the High Road, and its grand swing
from Stamford Hill into Edmonton. You do not
need a history book to tell you that this was one of
the great highways, where noble carriages, mail
coaches, and mounted men made great occasion.
Elizabeth—Elizabeth is a perfect nuisance to a
writer of local history—Elizabeth made many journeys to Tottenham, sometimes for a visit, sometimes
on her way to a hunting holiday—in Enfield Chase.

On this road halted James VI of Scotland on his

way to receive the English crown (Tottenham was pestered in those days with Scotch lords and rulers, as London has been pestered with them since). Many times, later, did James pass by, for he, too, found delight in Enfield Chase and at Theobalds, the home of Cecil, where he and the King of Denmark spent some wanton hours. Indiscreet memoirs of the period have fully confirmed the conjecture that this Scotch James was a pervert.

Through Tottenham, too, passed often that unfortunate set—Winter, Catesby, Fawkes, Meaze, and Rookwood on their way to White Webbs, at Enfield, where they met to co-ordinate their plans Unfortunately, they failed. Had they succeeded, instead of being carted round the streets in effigy, on November 5th, they would be honoured by processions of sanctimonious pilgrims bearing wreaths for their tombs in Westminster Abbey.

ELTHAM AND WOOLWICH

ELEGANT Eltham!

The slim, mincing syllables of the adjective mate very well with the rotund fat of the noun. Eltham retains to-day the physical features of a country village and much of its spirit ; for no suburb is more "suburban" than your country village, if by "suburban" one understands barrenness of mind, meanness of soul, pursuit of the paltry and disdain of the less fortunate. Old Sobersides and his friend Agelast have planted heavy feet in Eltham. It is the home of brokers, retired tradesmen and pious ladies who attend week-night services ; and it carries itself as such. It is complacent with prosperity ; greasily opulent ; not with the confident opulence of Mayfair, or the loud, candid opulence of the profiteer : it is stuck uncomfortably between the two.

Coming to it from the jocund precincts of its neighbour, Woolwich, one is sensible of a chill, as of cold boiled potatoes. The streets of Woolwich are gay with girls, but Eltham High Street and Court Road are prinked with "young ladies" and old matrons, wearing artless travesties of Bond

Street fashions. Genteel is not too strong a word for it. There is something tart to the palate in its atmosphere — a tincture of discontent. Its people would like to be something better than they already pretend to be. They look too unconvincingly prosperous. It is difficult to believe that people could be so actually prosperous as Eltham people look.

It has a story that clatters with armour and sword, and blazes with bugles and pageantry ; and under the shadow of these things waddle stockbrokers and retired bootmakers who have only seen the boots that themselves wear. This story has been told in a portly tome by Mr. Gregory, an Eltham schoolmaster, who, in his work, carried out successfully an attempt to teach his scholars English history through the story of their own village. Mr. Gregory is a native of Somerset, and it is quite in character that Eltham's history should have been dug from oblivion and recorded by a stranger. No Eltham "resident" cares a damn about Eltham's story. Mexican Oils are more his concern than the springs of History. Indeed, to-day's Elthamites are zealous in endeavours to hide the history away, to draw attention to their "desirable residences" and "commodious villas" ; but at this or that turn the posture and apparel of the florid past peep from behind the flimsy walls of to-day and shame the cold-potato-ism of the villas.

(How this man does love Eltham, doesn't he? Yes, I think he must have lived there.)

And what material it has! When Eltham Palace was a royal residence, great names appeared on its invitation list; and among those present, on divers occasions, were Erasmus, Sir Thomas More, Vandyck, Holbein, Wolsey, Chaucer, the Black Prince, the Earl of Essex, and, of course, the usual kings and princes, to whom a grateful nation offered the palace rent-free.

When John of France was taken prisoner by the Black Prince he was brought, in gentle captivity, to England, and Eltham Palace was his very comfortable gaol. The Trade Union of Kings arranged the comfort. With him came Froissart as secretary. The traceable homes and haunts of the old chronicler are so few that for this reason alone Eltham should be a treasured link with far-off things.

It was about 1360 that Edward III rebuilt and enlarged a scattered group of buildings which became Eltham Palace, and appointed it a Royal residence. From Edward III, then, to Charles I, every English sovereign, in unbroken succession, made here his home, and feasted and danced within the great banqueting hall, where now grow shoots of tender grass. At this palace took place a famous incident which Shakespeare, with his customary licence, has placed at Coventry—the departure of Henry Bolingbroke, Duke of Hereford, into banishment.

According to Holinshed, the Duke " took his leave of the King at Eltham, and took his journie into Calis." On his next visit to the Palace he came as Henry IV.

It was to the Palace that Henry V, flushed with the gory glory of Agincourt, brought his prisoners, and there lodged them, continuing, next day, his triumphal progress to London. Some years later, on Christmas Eve, 1515, arrived at the Palace gates another hero, then at the height of his triumphs, Cardinal Wolsey, summoned thither by his king. Following him a few hours later came Archbishop Warham, also by Royal summons. The one came to surrender the Chancellorship, the other to receive it ; and the little wooden cottages that stand now, as then, by the moat bridge, were my Lord Chancellor's lodgings.

Erasmus, introduced by Sir Thomas More (an Eltham landowner, of the manor of Well Hall), was a guest of Henry VII, and records a joyful hour spent with the young princes and the princess. So much enraptured was he with them that " I invoked the Muse that had long been absent, and composed an elegant Ode in Praise of England " for their delectation. John Evelyn, the dull diarist, was a frequent visitor ; Vandyck had rooms set aside for his use ; and one, Cornelius Debrell, was assigned a suite of apartments that he might expound and demonstrate to James I and " Stinie " his

marvellous new discovery (which is still being discovered) of the secret of perpetual motion.

Domesday Book refers to Alteham as being a
manor in the Kingdom of Kent, but the buildings
whose fragments now remain were erected by
Edward III. Originally, when in use as a Royal
residence, the estate comprised the capital mansion
house, the banqueting hall, the great hall, the chapel,
the keeper's house, and around the courtyard (now
a street of cottages and small provision shops) were
the buttery, the spicery, the pastry, the cole-house,
the slaughter-house, the bakehouse, and the scalding-
house. To-day all that remains is the banqueting
hall, the lodge, the moat, and the stone bridge.
The banqueting hall, very similar to the Great Hall
of Hampton Court, is a beautiful piece of work,
notable for its elegant simplicity. It is splendidly
lighted by twenty-two high windows, now empty
of glass and ragged with birds' nests. Beneath the
hall run many wonderful passages, giving egress to
the moat. It is not improbable that residents of
the Palace may from time to time have found it
convenient to leave by other than the front gate ;
certainly the passages are cunningly and solidly
constructed, and have survived the main mansion
by more than two centuries.

With the execution of Charles I came an end of
its glories. A few days after the catastrophe—or
act of justice, according to opinion—Parliament

found it necessary to send a Colonel Rich with a
body of troops to protect the Palace from plunderers.
With the Restoration it passed once more to the
Crown. But its days were done. It was never
again used as a residence by an English Sovereign.
After the pillagers had done their work, nothing
could revive its old charm and splendour, and it
was allowed to fall away. Indeed, the greater part
of it was actually destroyed; only the banqueting
hall was allowed to stand—it was found to be so
well adapted for a stable!

It may not be long, indeed, before the few forlorn
relics are altogether gone. They stand to-day amid
surroundings pastoral and ludicrous You approach
it by the very stone bridge constructed by Edward III
which leads over the sluggish green water of the
moat. On your right is a prospect of sloping fields,
with, on the sky line, the towers of the Crystal
Palace, and (save on very misty days) Westminster
Cathedral, St. Paul's, Big Ben, and the Victoria
Tower. On your left are straight roads of desirable
villa residences in glaring red-brick and stucco.
By the bridge a notice-board shouts at you the
searching question : " Why Pay Rent ? £10 Down
Makes You a Landlord." They do not ask for
money. They trust you! The age of chivalry is
not yet dead.

Other great names had association with Eltham
—Margaret Roper, John Lilburne, Sir Christopher

Hatton, Sherard, the horticulturist, Sir Thomas
Walsingham, Thomas Fairfax, Richard Bloomfield,
and Richard Jefferies—but Eltham does not care.
It is much more agitated over that mushroom
village which the War Office spawned upon it, near
Well Hall. Eltham has never forgiven Well Hall
for its impudence in seating itself at its elbow and
ignoring Eltham's pseudo-patrician frown.—" Cheap
workmen's villas, you know, dear—Clean their own
front steps, and go shopping on Saturday nights—
Thank goodness they go to Woolwich for the wretched
business." And fortunately, under the order of the
estate trustees, no intoxicating liquor may be sold
upon the Corbett Estate, which is the hamlet of
Well Hall ; and in the case of sickness in the house
the Well Hall man has to run three-quarters of a
mile for a bottle of brandy. Still, it keeps him in
order and serves to remind him that he is intruding
on a " select " suburb.

Froissart has left a tender record of his last visit
to the Palace. His object was to present to Richard
II a copy of his *Book of Loves*. Delightful Sir John !
Delighted Richard ! For " I showed him how that
it treated of matters of love, whereof the King was
very glad, and he gave it to Sir Richard Crendon
to bear into his secret chamber." The whole scene
is naïvely pictured in an old print, where Richard
is to be seen stretched upon a luxurious couch,
turning with delicate fingers the leaves of a handsome

tome, while Sir John sits upon a stool by the couch, and looks towards Richard with the timidly swanky air of the new author waiting for approbation.

I wonder what would happen, if one presented a *Book of Loves* to the Public Library of Eltham to-day ! I think the suetty mind of Eltham would fall upon the donor, and effectually extinguish in him any desire to repeat his public-spirited action. Eltham has suffered a vast money-change since those days into something sparse and too familiar.

At the Records Office you may find, among the papers relating to Eltham Palace a " Writ, discharging Geoffrey Chaucer, Clerk of His Majesty's Works " from repayment of a sum of ten pounds, the property of the King. This Geoffrey, it appears, was journeying, on horseback, from Westminster to Eltham, with the King's money ; and at Hatcham, near New Cross, he was set upon by four scurvy knaves, and robbed of his horse and all that he carried with him. He finished the journey on foot, told his story at the Palace, and was subsequently given a formal pardon for his misfortune. Shortly afterwards, however, Mr. Chaucer retired from his post, which seems to suggest that the matter of the ten pounds still rankled in the royal mind. So much the better, if it freed Mr. Chaucer from dangling after His Peevishness, and left him to amuse himself with the Wyf of Bath.

But such adventures are not now to be had at Eltham. They wouldn't be " allowed," I am sure.

I made my journey to Eltham in search of adventure, and found nothing. Adventure, I know, is not a commodity which can be obtained in sacks or chunks. You must make your adventure, if you want it. But in Eltham there are no materials out of which to make adventure; and even if you take your material with you, there is something in the atmosphere that re-acts on the material, and reduces a possible good dumpling of adventure to the consistency of bill-stickers' paste. Changing the metaphor, what you think shall be a jamboree declines into a spelling-bee.

Of Eltham I saw the unmellowed parish church —neither new nor old—under whose shadow rest Doggett, the comedian, of the " Coat and Badge," and Henry Seton Merriman—the Castle Hotel, the Public Library, the old Alms-houses, the Palace ruins, Well Hall manor house, the old houses of the courtyard, the new daughters of the retired provision merchant, the stout matrons of the Bombazine period, and the one reprobate of the place, who enters public-houses in broad daylight without looking to see if he is observed.

So I traded the fretful complacency of Eltham for the ornate clangours of Woolwich. Now Woolwich is a place. One may laugh in Woolwich, and catch adventure at every corner. I love the noise of men. That is why I love Woolwich. It does not attract at first sight. One could not love it for itself alone.

It possesses no external beauties, no excellences of line or feature, is tricked with no fair clothing. To love Woolwich one must love one's kind ; one must hold an instinct for humanity in its most crude expression — soldiers, sailors, policemen, costers. The very name of its station carries a primeval growl and clatter in its syllables—Woolwich Arsenal !

The essence of Woolwich is Beresford Square. It is Woolwich Bovrilized. At half an hour past noon the Arsenal gates open upon it, and it becomes the property of the Amalgamated Society of Engineers. In the evening it belongs to aimless, sauntering soldiers and their ladies. On Saturday nights it is a joyous country-town market-place, filled with cheapjacks, where the Cockney and the Kentish tongues are vigorously exchanged. On Sunday nights it is an arena where all the creeds of the world wrestle for supremacy : Salvation Army, Agnostic, Free Church, Socialist Brotherhood, Ethicalist, Calvinist, Comtist, Hegelian, Bolshevist—there they gather and dispute about it and about, and evermore are moved on by the over-worked police.

At all other times it is just Beresford Square, Woolwich, where you may buy the best of all fried potatoes. Woolwich is more than a suburb. It is a provincial town. Peopled by Cockneys, it yet stands apart from the metropolis ; belts of bare field sever it from London ; and the people seem to be conscious of this separation.

It has its own Co-operative Society, a bijou theatre adjoining the Barracks, called the Royal Garrison Theatre, a Gulliver music-hall, and " Barnard's "—otherwise the Theatre Royal, Woolwich. It is to Barnard's, by the waterside, that all earnest seekers óf entertainment go. I have spent some delightful evenings in its gallery. Barnard's was the last stronghold of the florid school of acting and drama. There one saw the full-blooded mellow dramas of twenty years ago : " The 10.30 Down Express," " Man and His Master," " London by Night," " The Still Alarm," " The Midnight Mail," " Harbour Lights," and so on. The audience, too, was of the old order. All that happened on the stage was of personal interest to the gallery.

" Leave 'im alone, you brute." " Grr—'it a woman ?—grr, yeh dirty dog ! " " Don't you go with 'im, gel—'e's a wrong 'un ! " " Look be'ind the curtain, yeh fool—look be'ind the curtain ! " " That Sir Gregory, y'know—I don't believe in 'im. I believe 'e'll turn out a bad 'un 'fore the play's over ! "

Which reminds me of what is, to me, a new story of Irving. Irving was rehearsing a play at the Lyceum, in which a real horse figured ; and an order for a horse was sent to Aldridge's. In due course an animal was brought to the scenery door and led to the stage. Irving walked round it.

" H'm. A fine animal. Very fine animal, indeed.

Tell me, is this animal likely to be at all nervous of the crowd and the footlights ? ''

" Oh, no, S'r 'Enry. 'E's bin on the stage before.''

" Oh, indeed ?   An actorr ? ''

" Oh, yes, S'r 'Enry. 'E's bin in ' Bound to Win 'and ' Sporting Luck ' and ' The Still Alarm,' and ——

" Oh, quite an actorr, quite an actorr.''

" Oh, yes, S'r 'Enry. Why, lars' yer 'e played with Mr. Tree through the run of Richard the Third. All excep' the lars' week, that is.''

" Oh, quite an actorr. Quite an actorr. Tell me, why didn't he play the last week ? ''

" Well, S'r 'Enry, as a matter o' fac', one night when Mr. Tree was on, fer the first time in his artistic career, 'e fergot 'isself, and lashed out and kicked Mr. Tree.''

" Oh, indeed ?   A critic, too ? ''

Wandering about the waterside alleys of Woolwich and its quaint wine-shops, I encountered my old friend Turnkettle—J. Turnkettle—Light Work Done With Horse and Van. Turnkettle is a Character, a Card, a Lad, a Nut—whatever word you please that designates one full of original whimsy and defiant idiosyncrasy.

He is physically and morally large, and his voice, when it first comes to you, comes as a shock, so meagre and Lilliputian is it. But his laugh holds double measure. It comes from the deeps and

shakes the furniture. He laughs at everything;
at himself, at the weather, at you, at the cost of
living, at Woolwich, at the horse-and-van, and with
everybody; in a laugh that resembles an American
college yell, loaded with various noise. It crashes
and jangles, and booms, and buzzes, and ends abruptly
in a nasal snort, as though surprised at itself. Even
the grotesque cauliflower fist that incloses his glass
cannot shield its contents from the disturbance of
the local air. His laugh seems to belong to Woolwich,
to be charged with Woolwich. Against it, all
other noises become wizened. That laugh and its
producer's prodigal magnanimity will relax the
most arctic social atmosphere. I have seen two
sworn enemies talk to one another in his company
You have but to hear him ask you:

" Well, how're things with you, boy ? " and follow
the question with his great laugh; and, whatever
answer you were about to make, you are compelled
to say that things are very well with you.

We spent a few raucous minutes in one of those
places where all men are equal; and then he said he
was doing nothing with the old brougham, and would
I go "tatts" with him. I said that I was always
ready to go "tatts" with anybody, but that on this
occasion I could go no farther than Eltham, as I
wished to return from there so as to take Lewisham
in my way. He said he would run me up, so we
went out. and, while he r dlnl ilied hi- I co 's feed-

bag, I stood watching a wandering minstrel with
a dulcimer, who was performing in the passage. I
am always drawn towards street entertainers; they
have that fascination for me that an empty salmon-
tin in the gutter has for an errand boy. He looked
up at Turnkettle, as we passed, but went on with
his work. His style with the sticks was pretty, and
I was about to address him, when he galloped hell-
for-leather through the coda of the " William Tell "
overture, gave a valedictory flourish of the hammers,
and cried: " Hi, Turney ! " Turnkettle looked
round. Nobody respects Turney ; everybody loves
him. " Where yeh going, boy ? "

" Eltham," replied Turney.

" Give us a lift, then. I want to get up to Catford.
There's nothing doing 'ere."

" Righto. Jump up."

So he jumped up, and we three—the Big
Turnkettle, the tiny dulcimer virtuoso, and the
traveller jogged into the drawing-room tranquilities
of Eltham. There Turney inquired of us if we would
not " take a little something," which we did ; and
I left the dulcimer man arranging his instrument
outside the Castle Hotel (what hopes !), and Turney
laughing at the Public Library.

I took the 'bus for Lewisham, and there met the
sailor who was proud of his mother. The 'bus was
full of Elthamites and Sidcuppians. They were a
sheep-faced lot, and hide-bound. The social atmo-

sphere was ice-bound. The sailor came aboard in
the Eltham Road like a high and gusty noon.

"Now we shan't be long. Oo—seats empty,
eh ? Scrumpshus. Ha ! "

With the explosive " Ha ! " he tumbled into a
seat and smiled broadly upon us.

" Leaf ! " he exclaimed. Then, with fine inconse-
quence : " Tea ! A meat tea. Sardines. 'Am.
Chips. Reddishes. Pancakes, too, shouldn't wonder.
All ready for me when I get 'ome. Kettle boiling.
Bren-butter all cut. And my ol' mother with the
teapot in 'er 'and. Ah," he gurgled, " I got a good
ol' mother, I 'ave. I 'ope you all got good ol'
mothers. I reckon you 'ave. You look as though
you 'ad. Eh ? "

We did not admit the existence of mothers, but
he was not abashed. " Great thing," he continued,
lyrically, " to 'ave a good ol' mother, isn't it ?
'Alf the battle, as they say, like. Don't you think
so, mate ? " He nudged his neighbour, a stout
member of the Old Proud. " You 'ad a good ol'
mother, I bet."

The Old Proud preened itself a little, examined
its boots, coughed, and looked through the
window.

The silence was frostbitten, and the sailor suddenly
was aware of it. " Hi, Nobby ! " to the conductor ;
" what's the matter with your mess to-day ? Got
the fantods, ain't they ? "

The saturnine man on the step gave a non-committal shrug.

"I tell 'em I got a good ol' mother, and they sniff."

"Well, they don't want to 'ear about yer ol' mother."

"Why not?"

"'Cos they don't."

"H'm." He pondered this for some moments; then his face lightened. "I know what it is. They think I'm drunk. Just 'cos I talk to 'em free-an'-easy, they think I'm drunk. That's what it is. But I ain't. I'm just 'appy. I ain't seen my ol' mother for three yers, and 'cos I tell 'em about it they think I'm drunk."

"Well, I dessay we all got good mothers, but we don't make a song about it."

"Why don't yeh?"

This somewhat flattened the conductor.

"Why don't yeh? Eh? Y'ought to. Ev'body that's got a good ol' mother oughter make a song about it."

"Ho, really? Nice thing it'd be, wouldn't it, if ev'body that's got a good ol' mother went about making a song of it. Nice thing to 'ave the ol' cart full inside and out, and ev'body making a song about their ol' mothers."

"You're right, Nobby," returned the sailor, "You're right. It would be a nice thing. We

ought to 'ave more of it. Wouldn't it cheer ev'body
up on your rowt and make 'em all remember what
good mothers they got. Eh? I wish I'd seen a
cartload like that yers ago, to remind me what a
good ol' mother I 'ad. I didn't know it till I got
away fer three yers. And now I'm going 'ome,
and she's writ and tell me all about the meat tea
what'll be ready fer me at sem o'clock. And 'cos
I want to tell somebody about it, they think I'm
drunk. It's all wrong."

"Oh, shut up about yer mother, fer 'eaven's
sake!" implored the conductor.

"Shan't. And what's more, you can't make me.
I ain't drunk, and I ain't misbe'aving. So you
can't put me off. Anybody'd think you was all
ashamed of 'aving good mothers. 'Ere—you, miss "
—he nudged a stout matron—" you 'ad a good
ol' mother, I bet."

He turned an imploring look upon her. The
corners of his lips twinkled. In a moment the
corners of her lips returned the twinkle. "Yes,
I had," she answered, with some embarrass-
ment.

"Hooray!" he yelled. "See? There's one of
yeh ain't ashamed to own it. There's one of yeh
simply bursting to make a song about 'er ol' mother.
I bet that lady's just dying to tell me that she 'ad
a better mother'n what I 'ad. Go on, miss. Let's
talk about our mothers. Shall us? Never mind

them. Your mother ever tell you nursery rhymes
—*This liddle pig went to market*—eh ? "

" Er—yes."

" Ah, I thought so. *And Mary, Mary quite
contrary*—eh ? "

" Banbury Cross ! " snapped the member of the
Old Proud.

" Hooray—'ere's another. 'E knows some. I bet
'e 'ad a good ol' mother. *Ride a cock-'orse to——*
My ol' mother used to sing that after bath-night
—Sat'dys."

" Quite so," murmured the Old Proud. " Quite
so. And *Water, water quench fire, Fire, fire burn
stick——*"

" Ah, you know 'em, guv'nor ! " He almost
danced in his seat. " 'Ow does it go ? *And the
cat began to kill the rat, and the rat began to gnaw the
rope, and the rope——*"

A greybeard in the corner volunteered. " And the
rope began to hang the butcher, and the butcher
began to kill the ox, and the ox began to——"

" That's it ! That's the stuff to give 'em. Lor
—'ow many yers since my ol' mother sang 'em to
me ! Takes you back a bit, don't it, guv'nor ? "

" H'm—er—yes—quite a while," murmured the
greybeard. " Quite a while." He looked vacantly
into space, and his voice fell to a croon of " cow
——fiddle——the moon."

" Ah, I tell yeh, soon's I get 'ome, and get outside

that meat tea, next thing I'm going to do is to set my ol' mother to singing 'em all over again. Every blessed one. What's this? Lewisham Road? This is mine. 'Nother two minutes, an' I'll be there. I can see the kettle boiling over. Oh, I got a good ol' mother, I 'ave. Bonswaw!"

He scrambled to the pavement, the conductor jerked the cord, and from the twilight followed a lusty voice: "Meat tea. . . . Cockle shells, all in a row."

And, as we laboured on, the conductor scratched his head and gazed about him, murmuring, "Up the clock. Up the clock. The clock struck one, and, and—— Oh, aw fez pliz!"

And so on to the Marquis of Granby.

FORTIS GREEN

I HAVE just been to see Fortis Green, and I don't believe it. I think it must have been a mirage. I think, if I go there to-morrow, I shall find that it and its people have vanished, and, like that insubstantial pageant, faded, left not a rack behind. It is so remote from every-dayliness; it is so improbable. It is a musical-comedy suburb; a place of Puckish humours. When I tell you what I found there, you will, I anticipate, tell me I am inventing.

Fortis Green is a diminutive suburb. It is a narrow strip of territory connecting East Finchley with Muswell Hill; but that narrow strip is richer in human interest than many acres of Bayswater or Westminster. It "appears" under the direction of the Hornsey Borough Council—an energetic and bright-eyed Council. When stray specks of dust appear on the roads, the water-carts are sent out. After a heavy fall of snow, men appear from nowhere to clear it away. Always it is well-kempt and natty.

The Council and its employees seem to follow the advice of Samuel Smiles, and take an interest in their job. When a fire breaks out, the fire-engine

arrives well within half-an-hour of the outbreak.
The Royal Borough of Kensington is not more
carefully tended.

Natty. I think that is just the word for Fortis
Green—place and people. It is bordered by trim
villas, their front gardens bright with lilac, laburnum,
chestnut, and jasmine bushes. It has pleasant
open spaces, named Coldfall Woods, from which
householders, in consideration of an annual payment,
may gather fuel for the winter-time against the
next coal-strike. Its women and children have a
natty appearance, and even its dogs wag their tails
with a pertness not found in the dogs of other suburbs.

But it is its cluster of human character that marks
it most sharply from other suburbs. Surely no
road of the same length is so fertile in queer company,
so pregnant with comedy and quaint idiosyncrasy.
There's the comic greengrocer. Passing his shop,
you might pass it as a suburban greengrocer's shop.
It isn't. It and its proprietor have wandered from
the vaudeville stage. Never was a pound of cherries
sold with so much badinage and "business." He
will sell you a marrow, as though the sale of a marrow
were a bustling Italian farce. An order for lettuce
is to him as the callboy's message to Leslie Henson.
There is nothing inherently funny about a cauliflower; yet this comic grocer of greens so touches
the vegetable with his humours as to invest it with
almost Rabelaisian grotesquerie.

Then there's the little beer-house, known as " Dolly's." Good company at " Dolly's," I warrant you. " Dolly " is a landlord of the substantial type. Watch him draw a pint of beer. It is a ceremony ; a solemn observance. None of your slapdash ways here, but amplitude of gesture and a reverential bearing of the filled tankard to the counter. Even the man who has a train to catch cannot disturb this function or accelerate it. It is Olympian.

Then there's the Fortis Green Literary and Debating Society, whose meetings are even more solemnly funny than those at St. Stephen's. Perhaps you know these societies ? Every self-respecting suburb owns a Literary Society, and, if you live in a suburb, you probably have not escaped membership. You know the order of business. You gather in a chilly parish hall, at eight o'clock of a chilly evening, and exchange murmurous remarks upon the evening's subject. Then the Chairman rises, passes more emphatic remarks upon the evening's subject, and concludes with : " And now, ladies and gentlemen, I will call upon Mr. Parkinson to give us his Paper on The Nobler Aspects of Lord Byron ; and as he is so well known among us as a serious student of that immortal singer, I am sure we are about to pass a very pleasant—and, I may say, profitable— evening. Mr. Parkinson ! "

The Chairman subsides ; you wriggle after a

comfortable position on your hard, straight-backed chair, and Mr. Parkinson, with a nervous cough, delivers to the Myrtle Park Literary Society, in reedy, complacent tones, his considered judgment on Byron.

The audiences of these societies are a mixed lot. The chairman is the curate; Mr. Parkinson, the platform hero of the evening, is a cashier at one of the local banks; and the regular attendants are elderly women, of means and no occupation, elderly men who have retired from business and now sort " intellectual " interests with gardening and golfing; and youthful clerks, typists, artisans, shop assistants —all bent on self-improvement, and some of them on the practice of letters.

They are to be found in every suburb—the same types forming the same groups, driven by the same motives. Every week, during the Autumn season, they meet; and to the Church Hall and the Public Library they flock with sleek delight to hear—not Sir Sidney Lee on Shakespeare, or Mr. William Archer on Ibsen, or Professor Arthur Thomson on Natural History, or Mr. Edmund Gosse on French Literature, or Miss Rebecca West on the Higher Criticism—-but Mr. Parkinson, Mr. Wilkins, Miss Diddlums on these subjects.

The bulk of the audience, the dabblers in the stream of literature, stand on the banks, gazing humbly upon those who have waded farther, and catching eagerly all that is tossed to them—the worn platitudes upon the worn novelists and essayists, the cobbled summaries of the messages of the philosophers, the solemn introductions to the beauties of established poets. But to the pupils and the teachers alike, these things are shockingly new. Neither pupil nor teacher is aware that they have been discovered before and that the self-same comments have been passed many, many times by others. The lecturer, on his side, does not care to know whether his audience has ever heard of Walter Pater or François Villon, or Croce. If he has chosen one of those subjects for his text, he will lecture on it ; and the audience, in their turn, will listen to him, because it is an " intellectual " subject ; and they will go home and read about it, so that, if he brings it forth again, they may be able to annoy his complacent bearing towards them by a few pointed references.

Apart from the meetings, the members exchange books and opinions with one another. The earnest ones, young and old, get together and arrange to read one book during the winter evenings, and to exchange letters on its moral and artistic value. I wonder whether Mr. Gibbon would have read with pleasure the letters that were exchanged in Myrtle Park last winter on his ponderous " Decline and Fall " ; whether Lord Byron would have been interested in the letters that followed Mr. Parkinson's

discourse on his " Nobler Aspects " ; whether Lord
Tennyson would have growled or grinned at the
correspondence arising from a reading by six Myrtle
Parkers of " The Princess," in the course of which
its Ethical Teaching was soberly discussed ; and
whether Miss Jane Austen would not have been
astonished at the high moral purpose which these
letter-writers discerned in " Pride and Prejudice " ?

The Papers are usually written and delivered by
the young ones—solemnly for the most part, with
an occasional elephantine jocosity, as one not at
ease in Zion. All are yearning to " write," and
they use the society as a training-ground for a
trial run of their efforts at the essay. Each has
his turn. The young labourer, the neat clerk, the
spinster typist—each is called upon for a Paper ;
and on the platform, whatever social distinctions
sever them elsewhere, they tread common ground.
Nervousness overcomes them, and they strive to
master it in the manner of their respective types ;
either by extreme diffidence or by dictatorial emphasis.
Some stutter and stumble, like Charles Lamb ; and
some roar and shock, like Roosevelt.

Yes, you may smile at them and their intellectual
adventures, but you must not laugh. The Literary
Society is as serious to them as the Royal Society
is to others. You see, they are all on the outside
of things. It is as stimulating to them to hear
their Curate read a Paper on " The Pilgrim's Pro-

gress," as for you to hear Quiller-Couch on Style, or Professor Gilbert Murray on Euripides; both you and they are listening to One Who Knows. Their Society is a peep through the gates of the garden of the mind. They want to be in it, and their leaders hold the key. They are the hangers-on of literature. They mess about with it, fumbling, without understanding, among its stores.

They are, to the informed bookman, as a baby with a box of paints is to the accomplished artist. But they have communal joys which the greater book-world never tastes. The excitement when one of them gets a poem into the local paper! The hysteria of congratulation when one gets something accepted and paid for by a real bookstall magazine!

" I will now ask Mr. Stamford Hill to give us his Paper on 'William Blake Considered as a Social Reformer.' You have all read Mr. Hill's masterly essay on Seaside Amusements in the current issue of the *Holiday Magazine*, and I am sure we shall listen with the deepest interest to a contributor to this popular magazine."

No jealousy; no bickering. Honest congratulations on the performance, with a reserved intent to surpass it. Why so many elders are found in these societies, I do not know. They never contribute a word to the discussions; and it is certain that no Paper has ever shocked them into thought or roused

them to an opinion. I think it is that they feel
they have missed some of the finer things, and as
Myrtle Park is their world, they wish to mix with
the intellectual set of that world.

" I always like to hear anything about books,"
says Mrs. Chomley Parke, stout and " comfortably
off." " I think books are so interesting, don't you ?
Are you fond of poetry ? I am."

The Society is, to her, the pivot of modern culture.
The lecturers are those interesting people—people
who have " done things." Alas, it is little that they
have done. The purpose is there, but the achievement. . . . You may, if you like, call it waste of
effort, misdirected energy on their part. You may
say that here is a thoroughly efficient bank clerk,
fully knowing his job, with every prospect of advance-
ment, spending the best of his brains in an effort
to become a mediocre essayist. You may point to
the capable manageress of a business staff turning
from the work that she can do to vain attempts
at work that she never will be able to do. Yet
therein they find their happiness. So who dare
complain ?

The printing of a set of verses (without payment)
in the local journal is a greater joy to the little
manageress than any vast success in her own business.
And the young bank clerk draws greater satisfaction
from appearing on an obscure platform and delivering his judgment on Byron to a few of his neighbours,

than he would draw from a sudden appointment to the managership of the Bank of England. Each of them has that slim ability to construct verses and phrases which, in George Wyndham's shrewd words, savours rather of deportment than of poesy; and because of it they become impatient of the work that they do so well, and beat vainly at gates that will never open to them.

Yet the effort is not wholly wasted. It brings them happiness and something more. It gives them the joy of books. It affords them the example of stronger characters. It teaches them self-expression and exercises their mental processes. It puts them through the discipline of concentrated thought. I am sure that Professor Gilbert Murray spends no greater care on the preparation of his lectures than does Mr. Parkinson on the preparation of his Papers for the Myrtle Park Literary Society. Such application and hard labour, bringing no material reward, compel admiration; and while many thousands flock nightly to witness the antics of maladroit acrobats reflected from a machine to a white curtain, I prefer to listen to the stumbling epithets and the unconscious plagiarisms by which Mr. Parkinson introduces me to Byron.

But Fortis Green is waiting to be inspected.

It chanced, on my visit to Fortis Green, that I fell in with a learned B.A.Cantab., whose confessed enthusiasms were his allotment and his beer. Of

Xenophon and Pliny he spoke as some men speak
of Mr. Lloyd George. With him I went on a Seeing-
Fortis-Green tour. I "rubbered." I saw the
police-station, the fire-station, and the new garage
with its public clock.

I saw his allotment. I listened, like a good tourist,
to the madrigals he made upon his marrows, and to
his lyrical outbursts upon the opulent beginnings of
his broad beans. I saw the home of Mr. Edwin
Drew, the poet. I saw Coldfall Wood. Then he
showed me " Dolly's," and all my interest in the
architectural and sylvan beauties of Fortis Green
was captured by the fauna of the district.

Will you believe that in one small enclosed space,
seven feet wide by two feet deep, I met a retired
Army man, who was with Burnaby on his ride to
Khiva ; a man who was with Beresford at Alexandria ;
a man who had hobnobbed with those almost legendary figures—George Leybourne, the Great Vance,
Jolly John Nash, and " The Perfect Cure "—a swarthy
Arabian, who kept a " general " shop ; a retired
Scotland Yard detective ; an ancient mariner who
had many times wind-jammed his way around the
world ; a truly staff-captain in full war-paint and
red tabs, who carried a savoury bag of fish-and-chips,
and ate from it ; and " Uncle Frank " ?

Perhaps you will not believe it. As I said above,
I can hardly believe it myself. Yet I know it happened. For I met the staff-captain in town day

5

or two ago, and he gave me directions for discovering the fish-shop where he had made his purchases, and spoke of it as selling the best fried fish in or out of London. Yes, he did. I dare say I met only a few of the delightful lads of this northern village ; no doubt there are many more. But with the arrival of "Uncle Frank," the walls of the cabin-saloon began to crack, and the air began to grow mephitic, and ribs tender.

I began to wonder whether the quaintest originals in London had agreed to settle at Fortis Green ; or whether there was something in the air of Fortis Green that changed a normal, dull man, making his home there, into an original. I think it must be the air. I am usually voted pretty dull company in the places I frequent : but on the occasion of my visit to Fortis Green, I was given, in this company of drolls, top marks as a merry fellow.

"Dolly's" bar is aptly named. In floor-space and cubic space it is the kind of bar you would find in a doll's house—if doll's-houses had bars. Everything is in miniature, except the tankards and the conversation. Conversation here is Brobdingnagian. This is compulsory, for two aged canaries hang in cages above the saloon. Many years have they been there, effectively obstructing, with their piercing voices, all coherent conversation. Often have serious debaters of affairs expressed the pious wish that some hungry generation would tread them

down ; but in Fortis Green everybody is so well
fed that the immortal birds are in no peril.

The prime character of the district, I think, is
" Uncle Frank." By his appearance and behaviour,
you would say that a star danced when he was born.
By his conversation, you would say that he was a
Senior Wrangler. He will discuss with you the
metaphysical basis of criticism, the influence of
geography upon history, the education of women,
and what's good for Goodwood. He is the leader
of all spontaneous goings-on, and a reference-book
for all arguments. He is the bright-eyed Tom-and-
Jerry of the place, who, with true avuncular gesture,
leads the lads into mischief, and, when it is done,
sees home his putative, obstreperous nephews.
Although old enough to know better, he regards
life as a beano. In a hard-worked, but efficient
phrase—he is the life and soul of the party. He
alone could bail Fortis Green from the horrid charge
of suburbanism, this ingenious farceur, this *espiègle*,
this Ariel of the tempestuous coat-tails.

In five minutes he had adopted me as his nephew,
and if your official uncles are crusty and pernickety,
send me a line, and I'll introduce you to an Uncle
who, I know, will Unc. as perfectly as the jolly
Uncle of your schooldays. It was at his request
that I wrote the lines that follow. He had asked
for a song, and I can't sing ; so I made this rondeau,
which he sang to an impromptu melody. to the

acute trepidation of the canaries. Unfortunately,
they survived it :

AT FORTIS GREEN

At Fortis Green the boys display
The joy of living all the day.
They drink their beer, and laugh and sing,
And carry on like anything,
Nor care a damn what people say.

Let others go in garb of grey,
And make November of their May ;
The pleasure's theirs. It's always Spring
                    At Fortis Green.

They show no shame at being gay,
These folk—they're always out to play.
And if you'd like to have your fling,
And lark about like Cole, the King,
Don't go to Paris. Come and stay
                    At Fortis Green.

EDMONTON

IT is usually difficult to traverse one London suburb without passing another's boundaries; so cunningly washed-in are their meeting points. You cannot walk round Stockwell without unwittingly trespassing on Clapham ; and often when you think you are at Manor Park you are treading the pavements of Forest Gate. Nevertheless, if your perceptions be reasonably acute, you are not long in discovering that you have entered a new country. There are subtle differences to be noted in dress, deportment and language ; in the aspects of the shops, the prices of the produce, and the manner of the tradesmen to their patrons. The fashions of Stamford Hill are never the fashions of Lee Green. Although Stoke Newington adjoins Kingsland, you could not mistake the one for the other. There is a type of face endemic to Hackney, whose people, on their part, find a strangeness in the demeanour of the man from Lavender Hill. The girls who parade Electric Avenue, Brixton, are as different in their qualities of charm and temperament from the girls of Grand Parade, Muswell Hill, as are the girls of Seville from the girls of Trondhjem.

Moving from one suburb to the other, then, I reach all the excitements of being " abroad." These strangers are driven by much the same motives as myself. They are buying cabbages and selling poisoned American meat, and going home to meals, and lining up for the show at the Electric Pavilion ; yet one cannot acknowledge them as one's own people. They are foreigners. They know nothing of my little corner. They do not know my High Street, or the baked potato man who has held a corner pitch for fifteen years, or the new store that has just opened with a tea room. They know nothing of the fury that is beating about the head of our progressive Councillor who has proposed an increase of expenditure on our public places ; and they would respond with no fervour to any comment of mine on the deplorable dilapidation of the tram-lines at the junction.

Though the main road of Tottenham flows natu-rally into the main road of Edmonton, the traveller cannot come unknowingly to Edmonton. They are severed from each other by a parting of the ways, which is actually marked Tottenham Boundary ; and at this point, High Road, Tottenham, becomes Fore Street, Edmonton.

The shop numbers of Tottenham mount grandly into the nine hundreds, and the solitary pedestrian beguiles his journey by speculating on their reaching the thousand. Alas ! they do not achieve it. Finding that they are approaching Edmonton, they become tired—they have my sympathy here—and give up the struggle at 920.

At once the serene Georgian residences of Tottenham—serene even in their present fallen estate of workshop and factory—give place to the agitated architecture of the mid-nineteenth century, wherein the Gothic influence of Albert battles with the classicism of Victoria.

Within the gates of Edmonton, I first sought out that famous tavern, " The Bell." I had heard about that, and had been recalling the stanzas of " John Gilpin " on the way. When I had found it, I wished I had not. True, it stands on the corner of a road, named Gilpin Grove, but it is a miserable, draggle-tailed road, with nothing of credit or renown about it.

As for " The Bell " itself, it is a cracked and battered old " Bell," a shabby copy of an East End pub. From it I received the first of many shocks of dismay that Edmonton gave me. After noting the preservation of W. A. Eaton in Tottenham shop-windows, I looked naturally for something that should celebrate the memory of the poet who celebrated the house : at least a portrait of Cowper, or a print of the house as it was, or an illustration of the poem. But no ; the owners ignore the man whose verses send pilgrims to their counters. The walls of the saloon bar bear only a coloured print of Victoria the Great and Good, and a discoloured cutting from an *Illustrated London News* of, I think, eight hundred years back.

I respectfully draw the attention of the landlords to this matter, if, as I believe, it lies within their province. The local authorities, less boorish in behaviour, have named two roads in association with Cowper ; Lamb's house, Bay Cottage, in Church Street, is, as it were, ear-marked for consideration ; and Keat's association with Edmonton, where he served his apprenticeship to the chemist, is suitably recorded in the Library.

" The Bell," let me add, is not alone in this cavalier treatment of its hero and benefactor. There are many taverns around London whose owners are so lacking in grace that they perceive not the grace in others. Town Halls and Public Libraries always make some effort to decorate their walls with old topographical prints, old portraits of local worthies, etc., but how many people, passing through a district, turn to its Town Hall or Public Library ? These attempts at celebration should rightly be supplemented by the owners of public places to which transient arrivals do go, such as taverns, restaurants, and tea-shops. In my own suburb, Highgate, are half-a-dozen old inns, each with a history and a long line of famous names in association with times past. Yet only one of these, " The Woodman," makes the slightest attempt at preserving the

traditions and the spirit of the house. There is
" The Flask," near the Grove, where Coleridge
resided. Coleridge frequently visited " The Flask,"
with parties of his visitors—Lamb, Hazlitt, Southey,
Haydon—and Hogarth made many studies here.
Yet the bars contain not one reference to this company ; no old prints of the village ; no relic of early
days ; no link with the honourable customers of
years gone. At " The Bull," on North Hill, George
Morland stayed for many months, and painted
pictures in settlement of his bills. Not so much as
the cheapest oleograph of a Morland picture in its
bar. The Gate-house on the Hill has in its lounge
a few old coaching prints, but no distinct record of
its past. The " Elephant and Castle " ignores its
rich story. " The Swan " at Tottenham has no
word to say of Isaac Walton, nor " The Peacock,"
Islington, of its crowded and coaching days. " The
Mother Redcap " does not know that Samuel Pepys
was a visitor ; and when I told the landlord of " The
Spotted Dog " at Upton Park that during the year
of the Great Plague the merchants of the Royal
Exchange met at his house to transact their business
he said " Really ? "

Of Edmonton itself ; well . . . I speak mildly
when I say that I was disappointed. I had heard
and read much of it. It has a story strung with
shining names. It appears and re-appears in song
and story and drama. And I never saw a place so

crestfallen, so down-at-heel, so bereft of self-esteem and so acquiescent in its degradation. You would hardly think that it stood upon the highway to the north. You would hardly think that it has shared with Tottenham all the pageantry of the road, all the changing colour of Tottenham's drama. You would hardly think that the author of *Endymion* lived with it; that Charles Lamb lies buried in it; that Dekker wrote one of his merriest plays about it.

It has the like to everything that Tottenham has; yet in its possession these things seem despicable. It has a variety theatre, as lugubrious in appearance as its streets. Apparently this hall opens twice nightly, and I suppose it has reasons for doing so. Yet its people seem incapable, not alone of rejoicing, but even of attaining to that spineless desperation that shapes the moods in which the Englishman goes to a music hall.

The place smells everywhere of the second-hand. On all sides one sees cast-off clothing, crazy furniture, old iron and broken crockery. It seems to have become a trollop through sheer lack of volition. Fore Street is a long, long street of shops; but on the day of my visit I saw no shoppers about, and I began to feel that I was walking in a haunted town. It seemed to me that all the population of Edmonton had turned shopkeepers—an appalling conception. Or else the shopkeepers, driven to madness by the new wave of economy, had murdered all their customers.

I called at one or two shops, just to solace their owners in their loneliness, and found that shopkeepers and innkeepers of this place were as unlike the shopkeepers and innkeepers of other suburbs, as Edmonton itself is unlike other suburbs. The joy of living and delight in labour were absent. They took no interest in their jobs. They were not shopkeepers and innkeepers, because they liked being shopkeepers and innkeepers. They were shopkeepers and innkeepers from dire necessity.

By this forlorn array of shops and Albertan villas, Fore Street straggles like a purposeless tramp to Ponder's End. Along it, half-empty tram cars grind their way half-heartedly to Waltham Cross, and all the way it presents the face of a drab—sealed cottages, waste corner-lots, and flat, tousled market-gardens, from which slinks the faint, gloomy odour of cabbage.

And this is Edmonton. Edmonton, that, three hundred years ago, was a busy country town many miles beyond London, yet well enough known to be chosen as the setting of two famous old plays —"The Merry Devil of Edmonton" (author, I think, unknown), and Dekker's and Ford's " Witch of Edmonton."

Here is wealth of story—Dekker, Ford, Cowper, Lamb, Keats. And what does Edmonton make of it ? Nothing. It seems to say : " Leave me alone. I know I'm an outcast Don't bother me. I'm down and out." It has the demeanour and aspect of a discharged convict.

One might find more of grace and soft outline in a north-country mining village. Its moral atmosphere is bleak and unfriendly. I spent three hours in its stark streets, and, though the day was warm, I was soon chilled and fatigued by the flat, frigid tones and the callous temper of the place. I wish Mr. Nevinson would do a painting of its soul. I think his obtuse angles would feel quite at home with such a subject.—Yet it was happy—once. Dekker says so, and pays tribute to :

> The nimble-footed youth of Edmonton
> That are so kind to call us up to-day
> With an high morris.

Little of this remains to-day. The youth of Edmonton lounge in premature senility at street corners, and the frolic grace and gesture of Dekker's times are no more. Only in Barrowfield Lane, by the level crossing, remain a few scattered stones of the original Edmonton—some gabled shops and houses—that Lamb and Keats may have seen.

But one other echo I caught there : something that, in my own mind, linked Edmonton again with Dekker. At mid-day I looked about for nourishment ; and, doing so, recalled a passage from Lamb —" How you would pry about at noon-tide for some decent house." In all these outer suburbs a mid-day meal is hard to come by. The Good Pull Up For Carmen and the afternoon tea-shop mark their limit in catering. Therefore, I was surprised and cheered to notice a house displaying an announcement of lunch at 1s. 6d. ; and announcing it by a word whose very flavour is a meal, and whose disappearance from tavern windows brought dismay to many—" A 1s. 6d. *Ordinary.*"

It is surely pitiful that a word that has lasted from the time of the seventh Henry to well into the twentieth century, and has gathered so rich a bouquet of association about it, should be dropped from the vocabulary of the streets. You may remember how knowingly Dekker writes in " The Gull's Horn Book," of " How A Gallant Should Behave Himself at an Ordinary"; and how largely it has figured in English literature throughout four centuries. Call it "*table d'hôte*", and all its savour is lost.

Had the place been evilly dirty, and the promise of the cooking a threat rather than a promise, I still would have gone there—because of that word. But it chanced that the place was reasonably clean, and the cooking without cause for complaint ; and the hour spent at that "Ordinary" remains my sole pleasant memory of Edmonton From its present sorrows I hurried away to recapture its past joys by reading again " The Witch of Edmonton."

CLAPHAM AND TOOTING

I STRAYED the other day without a map into a wilderness of strange men and women. I felt myself an alien, almost a pioneer, and I began to wish I had obeyed the exhortation of the old song and stuck to the tram-lines. But my trepidations were without cause. I found the natives harmless. They took no advantage my defencelessness. They did not seem angered at my intrusion. I was put to no peril. Nay, I was right cozenly entreated.

Perceiving a small building that bore some outward resemblance to certain buildings of my home-town, I entered, somewhat delicately, to inquire my best route to the highway. I had been inside this place barely ten seconds, when I was re-assured as to my venture. A patriarch of the tribe, whose duty apparently was that of ministering to those who called, gave me honorary rank and extended the hospitality of the village to me in these words:

" Wotteryavin, ole son ? "

" Ole son ! " What a welcome to the exhausted traveller in an unexplored country. I made suitable reply to this affable approach, and soon learned that

I was in Summers Town, and was free to go where I would about its precincts.

Summers Town is a dun, hapless, miry spot that lies land-locked between Wimbledon and Tooting. It seems to have been used by both as a sort of overflow, and is the draggle-tail end of Wimbledon and the tawdry beginnings of Tooting. Dreary tramcars, shorn of the lustre which is theirs at other points of their route, clatter sullenly through its worried streets, seemingly sick at heart and down-at-wheel. Throughout the sparse daylight they make the main road more miserable by their promise of "something doing;" a promise which is never fulfilled, for the natives do not use them during the day, and nobody visits Summers Town to see the room where Cromwell signed the pledge. Only late at night and at early morning, when nobody is looking, do they bear full and sleepy loads.

Humanity flourishes here, though. Ambition and aspiration, desires and dreams, are carefully nurtured, and grow the stronger perhaps by their hostile environment. The children, the dogs, the allotments, the little enterprises of the " mail-order " sort, furnish apt matter for evening discussion.

"Ah, you oughter 'ear my gel at the pianner. She ain't bin at it long, neither, but she's making a proper fist at it. Yerr ago she 'ad 'er first lesson. Yes—yerr ago come Pancake Day, it'll be. And now—why, she plays the Premier's Ballad and the

Ballot Egyptian—and, oo, anything. Seen anything of ole George lately ? "

" Oh, 'e's all right. Doing a little in the second-'and now, sort of side-line, y'know. And running a nice little business in teaching cabinet-making by post. Putting money away, too."

" Ah, 'e's got a business 'ead, ole George 'as. 'E alwis falls on 'is feet. 'Ow's your finches ? Mine'r a bit under the weather."

" Oh, mine'r a bit orf song, too. I say—'ere—'eard the one about the chap who went to Paris an' lorst 'is ticket ? "

And so on and so on. You are probably familiar with the elephantine jocosities and attenuated witticisms of the suburban bar. " Gorisms," as they are called in certain circles. I shan't explain that word. You are all Gorists at times, even the most brilliant of you ; but you will not understand the word unless you have been admitted to a little fraternity whose object is the detection of Gorism wherever it manifests itself.

From Summers Town one comes at last by long unwieldy roads to Tooting. It is perhaps worth while turning aside to Wandsworth. Wandsworth is famed for its gaol and its river, the Wandle, which has never been known to freeze. The Wandle was highly praised by Isaac Walton for its trout. It is to-day often condemned for its scum and its smell. The High Street of Wandsworth still has much the appearance of a village High Street, and many old houses still remain. In some of those alongside the river were housed the Huguenot refugees, who started there various industries, and built a church, on whose site now stands the Memorial Hall. Dutch settlers also made it their home, and carried on good business in brass pots and pans of their manufacture.

It was at Wandsworth that the foolery of the " Mayors of Garratt " was invented. Garratt— now covered by Garratt Lane—was then a hamlet ; and the idea of an annual election of a Mayor seems to have begun with some local inn-keepers. The candidates were usually street hawkers, eccentrics, or cripples. Each " Mayor " received the honour of a spurious knighthood, and the ceremony drew crowds of " the boys " from town, and usually ended in an alcoholic orgy. Sam Foote increased its popularity by his farce " The Mayor of Garratt."

At the other end of Garratt Lane lies Tooting. Yes, Tooting. I know what you're going to say. You're going to be facetious, and remind me of all the Pinero and Carton japes about Tooting. I can hear you enunciating its syllables—Tooting! Well I will not describe it as a pleasaunce. No doubt there are better places—Chelsea—West Kensington —Bedford Park. But what else could Tooting be, with that name ? It could not hold much of outward or visible grace. Professors of nomenclature have told us that the thing or person named borrows and develops character from the name. John just has to be honest, and Cecil must be weakly amiable. Gladys must be a flirt, and Mary sweet and placid. Camden Town is ordained to generate Camden Town-ness, and Cricklewood speaks of Helvetian chalets and half-made roads. So, in Tooting, the pilgrim finds what Tooting has promised him.

The very name speaks cold squalor, allotments, grubby brats, and a dilatory vestry. And all these things are there. At Lower Tooting, that is. At Upper Tooting we reach the rarefied slopes of culture ; villas at £100 a year, fur coats, Pekinese dogs, and weekly accounts with the baker, instead of cash down. One thing only wounds an Upper Tooting man more deeply than a letter addressed to him at Tooting, *tout court ;* and that is, a letter addressed to him at Balham.

Balham and Tooting hold much of cultural association. Mr. G. F. Monkshood, of Hatchard's, who lives there, reminds me of Defoe (who is remembered by Defoe Road and Selkirk Road), Fanny Burney, Sir Arthur Helps, Sir John Seeley, Thackeray (as a boy), and, later, Christie Murray, Ridgwell Cullum, the late Edgar Wilson, the artist, and B. W. Matz, founder of the Dickens Fellowship, who keeps there his wonderful and priceless Dickens Room. May I also mention, among those present, two Thomas Burkes—one, a singer, the other — well, him you may describe as you please.

From Lower Tooting the road ascends gradually
to Balham, and again from Balham to Clapham
Common. Of Tooting, my pocket-guide to London
says (appropriately enough, on page 222) that it
stands on the Epsom Road, and is reached by train
and tramcar, and that the name is derived from
Teut, the heathen god.

This has a distinctly German touch about it;
and, when considered with the ancient name of
Balham—Belge-ham—helps me to understand why
Balham was flooded in 1914 by droves of Belgian
refugees (who carefully avoided Teuting). They
appeared to regard Balham—or Belgeham—as their
own property, judging by the treatment they gave
to houses which were kindly loaned to them. The
domestic habits of the German may be frequent,
and painful, and free, but I fancy they must
have been acquired from the Belgians. Speak as
you find, of course; and praise where praise is due;
and I am sure nobody could outdo these particular
Belgians in their special line.

Balham High Road, the shopping centre, affords,
on a bright morning, a pleasing picture to the student
of statistics. Clearly the monitions of Father Bernard
Vaughan are not required in Balham. One would
scarcely believe that one small suburb could produce
so many bonny babies, year by year. At mid-
morning the pavement resembles the track of an
obstacle race, what with perambulators and push-

carts, loaded with obese and complacent babies, and other babies feeling their feet around their mothers' skirts. The man in a hurry must either walk in the road, or have his trousers fringed and frayed by the spokes of an everlasting procession and counter-procession of His Majesty's carriages. " Why don't you look where you're going ? Clumsy great thing, you ! Diddums nasty old man knock-ums pushcarts, then, diddums ? "

The shops of Balham are bright and bold, and the shoppers don't seem to have done so badly out of the war. If they have, they are keeping very quiet about it. At Tooting, where the shops are humbler and ill-stocked with poor produce, they don't seem to have done so well, and they are not quiet about it. The various bodies of ex-fighting men have very active branches at Tooting. The shops alone, by comparison with those at Balham, are enough to make them active. On the analogy of the menagerie-keeper's description of the wild cat, the case might be presented something like this :

" We 'ave 'ere, ladies and gentlemen, the wild ex-soldier from Wipers. 'E useter be a fine upstanding young lad, eating 'is four squares a day and making good money. Now, 'e don't make no money at all."

" Don't make no money ? How does he get a living, then ? "

" 'E *don't* get a living. That's what makes 'im wild ! "

At Nightingale Lane we come to Clapham Common, whose borders are so rich in ancient story that the two books on Old Clapham have chronicled only a portion of it. Across the Common, on the South Side, the beautiful small houses built by Christopher Wren may still be seen; but at a distance they are dwarfed by a block of gigantic four-storied houses of the stately Victorian period. At one of the Wren houses Thomas Hood received his early education, and celebrated the school in his " Ode on a Distant Prospect of Clapham Academy." In another, Macaulay lived as a boy, played lonely games on the Common, and attended the not very beautiful church, of which he spoke with the freedom of an old friend: " I love it . . . I love even that absurd painted window. . . ." I, too, have a soft spot for Clapham; for it was at Clapham, as a youth, that I made my first discovery of literature, and my first efforts at writing. There I gathered together my first " library." I suppose you all possess a library ?

I don't mean those ponderous properties of the wealthy, which are housed in one sombre room, having the appearance of a household store-cupboard or a wine-cellar; but the collection of books which has grown under its owner's careful nurturing, and is enriched by no more than two volumes at a time. Its owner knows a delight from which the lordly librarian is barred: the delight of reviewing his volumes and dilating upon the sacrifices by which each was added to his shelves. Each has its memories, and most fragrant are the memories that cling to the parent-volumes of the collection ; those hardly-purchased forerunners that record his first efforts at book buying.

Most bookmen cherish these worn favourites. There is a novelist known to me who now possesses rare editions, full sets, fine bindings, and other dainties of the bibliophile. But his dearest volumes stand on the shoulder-high shelf by his desk—half a dozen grubby volumes of the Chandos Classics, from which, when held in the fretful toils of the factory bench, he first tasted the good dry wine of literature.

My own university was the Scott Library and the Canterbury Poets ; and my earliest purchases were Poe, Keats, Shelley, Wordsworth, Wendell Holmes, Cowper, Gray, and de Quincey. I was about sixteen when I first " discovered " literature, and was then living in Clapham and labouring, as a junior clerk, in the City. It was near the time when the first number of the *Book Monthly* appeared on the book-stalls. By walking home to Clapham on two evenings, and saving the tram fare, I was able to buy that first number. Why I was moved to buy it, I cannot say.

At that time the monthly illustrated magazines and the weekly " home " papers had served me

very well. I suspect that I had a sneaking desire
to shine against the lumpy and threadbare minds
of my office colleagues who, I was beginning to
realize, irritated me. Perhaps I wanted to high-
browbeat them. Anyway, I bought that number
and read it line by line. At about the same time
T. P.'s Weekly made its first appearance, and that
also I bought. Then I started on my tour of discovery. Mr. James Milne and Mr. T. P. O'Connor
together flung open to me the gates of the realms
of gold ; and through them I plodded, aided only
by an occasional sign-post which the good Mr. Milne
or the good Mr. O'Connor erected for my welfare.

My first purchases were poetry, bought with
foregone midday meals. I do not know why poetry
should have taken my fancy. Maybe one of my
guides made poetry his initial direction. Maybe
I thought poetry somewhat more " intellectual "
than prose. Anyway, the Canterbury Poets were
my first books. Each volume contained, at the
end, a full list of the series, and one led to another.
Instinctively I knew that Shelley was more considered than Eliza Cook, and that Sir Thomas Browne
wrote better prose than Mrs. Henry Wood ; but
beyond that I was uninformed.

I bought without reason or judgment ; it was
enough for me that a book was included among
" standard works." A " standard work " was clearly
a thing to have, if only to shy at the heads of those

who read the serials in their newspapers. I became
a guzzler of literature. I wolfed it down without
mastication or assimilation. I was a book-hog. I
followed Keats and Shelley with Bret Harte and
Adam Lindsay Gordon. Oliver Wendell Holmes
made one mouthful with Heine and Dante ; and
George Gissing went down with Otway and other
Restoration dramatists.

The times were good to me. The "Canterbury
Poets" were 9d. each ; the "Scott Library" (prose)
1s. 2d. Grant Richards was just beginning his
"World's Classics" at 1s. Cassell's "National
Library" was 8d., and Routledge had a 6d. cloth-
bound series. I am sorry for the youth of to-day.
The cheapest editions are now 2s., and Charing Cross
Road has heavily revised its terms. The ill-paid boy
(yes, there are still some ill-paid boys) who has "dis-
covered" literature is now barred from it, or driven
to that sad counterfeit of book-delight, the Public
Lending Library.

I cannot here publicly disclose by what shift these
books were acquired. It is one of the things one
doesn't talk about. But at slow intervals I gathered
about fifteen "standard works," and when I wasn't
reading them I was looking at them. I would walk
about Clapham Common in November dusks with
de Quincey in my pocket. I would carry Chatterton
down Newgate Street to Holborn. I read Herrick
(The World's Classics edition) in the Strand ; and

Cheapside and Poultry, through which my office duties took me every day, became interesting, because Thomas Hood was born in Poultry.

I soon developed " opinions." Tennyson and Dickens were good enough for those who didn't know any better. You see, I had long been familiar with them ; our school reading-books had sickened me of them. Tennyson was a so-so poet, and all sorts of people read Dickens and understood him. Whereas, I was alone in reading Herrick and Marlowe and Otway and Wendell Holmes.

This violent gluttony of books quickly produced an uncomfortable feeling. It wasn't long before something happened. At sixteen I wrote a short story. And I sold it. A small " home " journal called *Spare Moments* offered a weekly prize of one guinea for the best story sent in. For three months after its dispatch I heard nothing, and assumed that it had been lost or not delivered, and forgot it. Editors were kings, and I had gathered from my reading of my literary papers that it was sacrilege to approach an editor on the subject of MSS. Then one morning arrived an envelope and a cheque for one guinea.

I rejoiced, not so much at the novelty of being printed, as that I could now justify myself in the eyes of those who misregarded my lust for " standard works." In my City office I was one day surreptitiously reading the *Book Monthly* under a blotting pad. The head clerk returned unexpectedly from lunch.

"What you got there, me boy?"

"Nothing," I replied. "Only one of the literary monthlies."

"Literary monthlies!" Mr. Milne should have heard the torrent of scorn that ran through those syllables. "Literary monthlies. You don't want to waste your time on that kind of thing, me boy. You want to read things that'll get you *on*. . . . Here, I've got a book in my desk that's been of endless use to me. I'll lend you that—it'll do you twenty times more good than poring over that kind of thing."

And he lent me a *Manual of Office Routine and Procedure.*

Well, I was inflated by that story in *Spare Moments* ; and half-shyly, half-swankily I produced it to him in justification of my "literary monthly."

"What's this?" he asked.

I indicated the story, with my name to it.

"Well, what about the story?"

"Nothing," I said. "Only, I . . . I wrote it."

He tossed the paper away. "Come, come, me boy, don't come wasting my time with silly fibs like that. You ought to be ashamed of yourself."

I was. I don't know why. But I was ; and thereafter I brought no "standard works" to the office ; or, if I did, kept them privily in my overcoat. But I had begun. I had had a story printed, and I had a shelf of sixteen poets and essayists, and each week new poets and essayists were to be discovered. Many times, I am sorry to say, the contents of that shelf disappeared, sometimes to be replaced by similar volumes, sometimes replaced by new discoveries. But those first purchases are gone; they went, before I left Clapham, to second-hand booksellers long ago, when the times pressed. I have not now my Herrick and Poe, in the World's Classics; I lack my Shelley, Wordsworth, and Keats, in the Canterbury Poets; and I miss the pleasant sage-green and gilt of the Scott Library. They served me well, and herewith I give thanks to their publishers who so lightly priced them.

To me, the most moving scene of Clapham's history was the death of Hardicanute on the Common, dim centuries past, after doing his duty too well at a wedding feast. Perhaps that is why Clapham is so well furnished with old hostelries. Of these, the seniors are "The Windmill," on the Common, with its old carriage-drive, and " The Cock," by the Old Town, first built in the sixteenth century. The " Plough " Inn, now a great junction for the tramways, still has its old yard, hinting at coaching times. This yard, once an inn yard, was later the stable of the old horse-driven tramcars, and is now a garage.

My own recollections of Clapham go back to

boyhood, when the Common and its many ponds were my Saturday delight. Another past delight —past, since the coming of the motor—was Derby Night, when one went to the High Street to watch the return procession of multifarious vehicles, from the elaborate four-in-hand to the donkey-chaise, comprising, between those points, the brewer's dray, with upturned barrels, the coal cart, furnished with the kitchen chairs, the cat's-meat cart, the country wagon, the hansom, the growler, the brougham, the landau, the fish-cart, the milk-float, the—oh, every vehicle ever seen on the London streets, and many that had been dug from remote yards where they had rested since the railways began.

Then the High Street was a fair ground, with squirters, ticklers, air balloons, all-the-fun-o'-the-fair, long noses, Guy Fawkes masks, streamers, paper hats—and " Throw out yer mouldy coppers ! " Then, each returning party raked their minds for some new device wherewith to brighten the road. They changed hats, of course, and put some of the harness on the old woman, and dressed the donkey in camisole and knickers, and painted their faces, and made genial discord upon those imported musical instruments which are the voice of merry-making England—the accordion and the mouth harmonica, and—well, went mad in a way that in these times is frowned upon.

Vulgar ? Yes ; so is Dickens ; so is Fielding.

STOKE NEWINGTON TO HARRINGAY

THAT was a good day when I first performed a task that I had long deferred : when I tracked Green Lanes from its humble origin at Newington Green to its end amid the vast plain of Enfield Chase, Middlesex. It was a day in April, and April was in the day. As I boarded the car that was to carry me to Newington, the sun shone through an austere breeze, and I said to myself that I would have adventure. I was journeying into a strange country. I would make abrupt and hazardous acquaintance with strange men. I would receive good messages from nameless bright countenances. I would see new frocks, new hats on new crowns of hair, new shops, new streets, new methods of trade, new attitudes to life, new gestures ; and I would enrich myself by barter of talk and courtesies of the road.

Like every self-respecting suburb, Stoke Newington is well-to-do in the matter of inns. When James VI of Scotland came to London to receive the English crown, he was met here by my Lord Mayor, and the " Three Crowns," at the corner of Church Street, stands as a memorial of that occasion. " The

Jolly Butchers," associated with an early Duchess
of Devonshire, is a good house, too ; but the best
of them is the " Weaver's Arms," a terminus for
the old-time horse-'buses, and even now not without
its flavour of whip and harness. Its collection of
early Hogarth prints shocks and delights one, so
rarely is such taste displayed. Your London landlord is usually content to decorate his walls with
gawky, banal devices of brewers and distillers ;
wretched process work, out of register, enclosed in
gilt frames as bold and bellying as an alderman.
It was a pleasure to sit among these prints : the
worst of beverages would drink well in such company.

As I sat, I remembered that in Church Street,
across the road, Defoe lived, and it is held, there
wrote part of *Robinson Crusoe* ; that Northumberland,
the young lover of Anne Boleyn, dated from here
his humble renunciation of the lady to his royal
master ; that Samuel Rogers was born here ; that
Mrs. Barbauld, remembered now by one poem which
Wordsworth envied, lived here as wife of the Presby-
terian minister ; that Edgar Allan Poe was here
at school ; and that it has two parish churches in
the same street.

I then went out and looked round. The solid
houses of Newington Green still breathe a self-satisfied
Victorian air. They seem to fold white hands across
lace stomachers, and never to have heard of silk
stockings. One thinks here on Sarah Smyth, her

sampler, on silver tea-sets, on keepsakes, and amulets, and Sheraton bookcases.

But in the High Street the air blows keen and strong. The New North Road here shakes itself free of the East End and becomes broad and spacious. One has a sense of looking through the open window of London. Here is a land of parks and greenery —Mildmay Park, Abney Park, Clissold Park. Of these, Clissold only is a park in fact. Abney Park is a cemetery, named after Sir Thomas Abney, the benefactor of Isaac Watts, whose *Divine and Moral Songs* were forced into us in youth ; Mildmay Park is mainly an array of villas, which, like the poetry of Rowbotham, the modern Homer, are stiff, but not unpleasing. The borough's general aspects are wide, for Leyton Marsh, Hackney Marsh, and Victoria Park lie on the east, between it and the crowded acres of Walthamstow and Leytonstone ; and its north-east looks upon Tottenham marshes and the reservoirs.

It displays, like most northern suburbs, signs of good management. These districts are so far in advance of those of the other side of the river that they support a local daily—the *Islington Daily Gazette*. They demand, too, and get good value for their rates. Nowhere in the South will you find boroughs so well-kept and garnished.

To the traveller from the flats of Shoreditch and the dolours of Dalston its air yields a certain bite ;

The very name Dalston has a cold, gritty sound to it, quite out of harmony with flowers. I think they must hold in their own hearts some secret source of breeze and sunshine. Indeed, I am sure they do; for not without some such private hoard of joy could they, in these ungentle places, remain so affable, even cordial to the casual wayfarer.

The tradesmen of these parts sell their fruit and vegetables at a penny or twopence lower than the prices ruling at Stoke Newington and Stamford Hill: a fact which by itself conveys to the informed observer, who knows one of these districts, the essential spirit of the others. So the knowing ones of Stoke Newington board the car and come to Kingsland and Dalston for cheap provender; and the tired shopmen of these markets, when they feel the need of a breath of fresh air, take the car to Stoke Newington; an example of that interchange of courtesies between suburbs which I am anxious to extend. There, they may be blown free of the dust of Dalston, and, from the top of the car, may look across the shingle of roofs that sweeps down to the green pastures of Hertfordshire.

There, the High Street by day is full of shops and wheels, and sounding horns, and severe endeavour; and in the crisp evenings it is a grand parade.

> When Ciss comes home from typing,
> And Tom has earned repose,
> Then merrily sounds the tabor,
> And merrily move their toes.

But there is a fly in the ointment. There is a nasty something underlying the jam. There is a rift in the lute. Stoke Newington's scutcheon carries a bar sinister. Opposite Abney Park, and just off the High Street, stands a hideous block of buildings named Gibson Gardens. If ever you hear that they have been burned down, you will know that I did it. This building is capped by a sign more hideous, reading :

THE METROPOLITAN ASSOCIATION
FOR IMPROVING THE DWELLINGS OF
THE INDUSTRIOUS CLASSES.

A few yards away a Female Guardian Society has quarters. A Salvation Army citadel hurts the eye on the right, and bands of thin-faced Brothers and Sisters lurk near by.

Now what's the matter with the people of Stoke Newington that they require such a deuce of a lot of looking after ? Who inspired so many futilitarians to direct their campaigns at Stoke Newington ? I don't believe its folk are in such a state of moral turpitude as to require the extreme ministrations of such bodies. I would like to know whether these people are here by invitation, or whether they are intruders, hanging about with the object of inoculating the less perfect with their own lymph of perfection. Note the adjective in the self-advertisement of the founders of Gibson's gloomy Gardens. " Industrious " classes Most improvers work in a wider sphere, and seek to polish and improve the whole vast army of industrials. Not so the M.A.I.D.I.C. Only the nose-to-the-grindstone man for them, though if Cobbett and Sam Smiles and other guides to success may be cited as authorities, this fellow needs no external aids ; his broadcloth merits will of themselves carry him to the Mansion House. Nowhere have I seen a hundred square yards so loaded with ugly well-doing. Why, oh, why cannot man attain moral rectitude without contracting the mania to mould all other men to his pattern ? Stoke Newington seems to say to me through these blazoned signs of virtue : " You don't want to be improved, don't you ? Then you jolly well shall. Just wait till we catch you. We'll learn you ! "

Under these uncharitable eyes I began to be at first depressed, then alarmed. Suppose, I thought, someone, oozing this improvident perfection, is hanging about street corners to pounce upon stray wanderers and improve them? Suppose he nabs me ? So I turned hastily aside, and darted away to take another refreshing look at the Hogarth prints, and to wonder why hard-faced virgins and morbid missionaries never adopt the Hogarth method of improving.

I was still inspecting them when a voice interrupted me.

" Got yer 'olidays, mate ? " The words were snapped at me from the bar.

I always answer " Yes," when taken aback by
a question. I said it on this occasion.

" That's the style. Just a good time fer 'olidays.
In the City, I suppose ? " He might have been
giving me ten rounds rapid.

I nodded.

" Ah ! I used to be. Couldn't stand office work,
though. Soon's I got me ticket, I started on me
out-o'-work Dole. Just drawn this week's. Want
to buy a stud ? "

I turned fully round then and inspected him.
He was a little stout-built fellow, with sharp lips
and tiny twinkling eyes, which softened the snap
of his sentences. The worse half of a Woodbine
was gummed to his lower lip. He was wearing an
Army issue civilian suit, and carried a little wooden
attaché case. As our glances met I saw that he
was bursting for companionship. He stood stiffly
before me, arms down, and appealed. I responded.

" I've got quite a lot of studs," I said. " That
all you're carrying ? "

" All ? Jumping rabbits ! I should think not.
I got everything here," he went on, patting the
case. " Everything in the world I got 'ere. In a
manner of speaking, that is. . . . 'Ere, 'ave a look.
See if there's anything you fancy." He put the
case on the lounge, and opened it. " There y'are.
'Ave a look. That's my job now. No more office
for me. Something that takes you out. That's

what I went for. No hours. No indoor work. Just
go where yeh like, and pick up what yeh can. I
bin free munce on this now, and wherever I bin I
can always go again. When I was out at the front
I wrote to the missus, and I says I'll go no more
a-roaming, or words to that effeck. But when I
got back I sung a different song. Up an' down the
City Road, in and out the ' Eagle '; that's my
song now."

"It's a very good song," I said. "Do you sing
it all day ? "

"Sing ? Me ? I never done nothing else in
Frawnce. The boys wouldn't never give me no
rest. Listen."

He flourished an arm, danced a few steps, and
sang in a muffled baritone :

> "Oh who will roam the streets with me,
>   From Strand to Camberwell ?
> Oh who will buy a ring from me
>   To give unto his gel ?
> I've diamond pins and solitaires
>   And all such things as these ;
> And if I ain't got what you want
>   You must be hard to please ! "

"There ! What d'ye think of that ? I made
that up meself. . . . Oh, yes, I made up a lot of
poitry for our corps magazine. Don't yer want to
buy a stud ? "

"Not at present," I said. "But I'll tell you
what," I added, for I had caught a sudden joy of
the fellow , " I ll answer your song with Yes. *I'll*

roam the streets with you. I was just starting on a roam when you spoke."

" Where to ? "

" To the very end of Green Lanes."

" 'Strewth ! Where's that ? Country ? I ain't going to no countrified places."

" No ; there's no country until you get to Southgate."

" Ah, that's all right, then. Any chance of doing a bit of biz. on the way ? "

" I wouldn't wonder," I said.

" Righto. Then if my company ain't going to inconvenience you in no way, I'll come with you. Sure you don't want to buy a stud ? "

" Quite sure at present. But your case may be useful before the day's out."

" Good. If you can't book an order, you can sometimes make a friend. 'Tain't often you can do both. Now we'll close 'er up, and I'm ready Giss a fag, ole man."

So we started. We had fallen at once into easy comradeship, without the diffidences and reticences of nice people, and we went briskly across the Green to the mouth of our road. We were of one mind, and asked nothing of each other but light talk and a swinging leg. Past Clissold Park we soon sighted the huge towers of the reservoirs of the New River Company, and the many-roomed villas of Highbury New Park of the kind described by house agents as

" substantial," to mark them, no doubt, from the baseless fabric of the homes of Holloway. The New River is that same old river which, constructed by Hugh Myddleton, and financed by James I, brought Myddleton an empty knighthood and material ruin, and immense prosperity to shareholders.

The industrious William Howitt, in his *Northern Heights*, tells a sorry story of the parsimony of the company towards Myddleton's family. In the middle of his enterprise Myddleton, having used all his capital, appealed to the wealthy City merchants. None would aid him. James came to the rescue and advanced half the total expense in return for half the shares. Once the thing was done, and its success was assured, the merchants stepped in to buy. Certain small grants were conferred on some members of the family for some years, but soon these ceased entirely ; and the statue of Myddleton at Islington Green is regarded as sufficient token of London's gratitude to the man who brought pure water to the city.

From " The Manor House," where Seven Sisters Road crosses Green Lanes, the way lies straight to Harringay and Hornsey. Harringay, I learn from the local guide, " is and has been for many years a suburb with a distinct individuality of its own. . . . Altogether, Harringay may be described as a bright and cheerful suburb." In possessing an individuality of its own it does not differ from any

other suburb. I confirm the " bright and cheerful " ;
though, if you come to Harringay by train, you
will alight at a station which it shares with Green
Lanes, and the view from the platform may damp
your simple faith in guide-books. But views from
stations are not a fair test of a town's charm. Think
of the view of London from Euston or Liverpool Street.

I quoted the guide-book to my companion.
" Bright and cheerful, eh ? " he echoed. " Well, I
don't mind if it ain't. Put me down in the miser-
ablest place, and I'll guarantee to make it bright and
cheerful 'fore I finished with it. I'll set 'em alight ! "

With half-an-hour's acquaintance with him I
believed him ; and I suffered an earnest desire to
lead him at once to my own too stately and bourgeois
road, Shepherd's Hill, and let him set that alight.
Shepherd's Hill is even more oppressive than Bayswater. It is a wide, clean thoroughfare, bordered
by bright trees. It has large comfortable houses,
whose sweeping front gardens scatter laburnum and
lilac blossoms along the pavements. It is open to
north, east, and south, and big breezes beat about
it. People ought to give thanks publicly for living
here. Yet never do you hear a sound from these
houses. Never have I seen man, woman, or child
enter or leave them. Never have I heard a voice
in song. Never have I heard a child laugh or cry.
Never have I seen a young man coming home late,
or a young girl with her boy. Not a sign of human

life is to be seen, save tradesmen and their carts.
Hideous stillness broods over all. Providence has
given these people pleasant bread, and they accept
it with a scowl, as though it were a stone That
mean, middle-class quality of "reserve" has led
its people to applaud, as something in itself admir-
able, a sulky demeanour towards the outer world.
What do these poor creatures at Highgate? Highgate, whose air was coloured and enriched by Coleridge,
George Morland, Hogarth, Lamb, Hazlitt, George
Eliot, Faraday, and Tom Sayers. There are plenty
of places whither these automata might take their
brutal refinements—Cromwell Road, Bayswater, St.
John's Wood—but to Highgate, the field of poets
and artists who knew how to live and how to give
thanks, they belong as fitly as a Calvinist at carnival.
They are a disagreeable excrescence.

They are the middle-class; and the middle-class,
in every corner, has for centuries been a drag on
progress. It has jumped with its well-made boots
upon all new ideas and very heavily upon all ideals.
The middle-class scoffed at the railway. The
middle-class refused to believe the motor-car when
it saw it. The middle-class ridiculed the idea of
the telegraph and of aviation. And the extent of
its hatred of art is disclosed at Mudie's and the
Royal Academy. You may have noticed that,
wherever the singers and the artists go, these people
of the lumpy minds follow and drive the artist away.

They have killed St. John's Wood. They have killed Maida Vale. Slowly they are getting their strangling fingers on Chelsea. There has been much talk lately of a Middle-Class Defence Union. Believe me, these people need no Union for their defence. They are quite capable of looking after themselves. Wherever they have seen anything that better judges have pronounced good, they have stolen it. In a century or so they have stolen from the labouring class more than the feudal lords stole in many centuries. They stole for their sons Eton College, Westminster, Winchester, and Charterhouse, originally founded for poor scholars ; and they stole fifty other schools and institutions dedicated to the impoverished. But from these stolen goods they have derived little benefit. The vacuity and the fumbling dishonesty that disfigure modern politics is traceable to the fact that seventy per cent of the members of " my faithful Commons " spring from the middle-class and its stolen colleges.

And there they are, smug and smirking, on Shepherd's Hill. I would like to walk down that hill with a trumpet, a drum, a pair of cymbals, and a megaphone, and shout beneath all windows : " Oh, good people, look out from your screened windows and rejoice. Come out of your doors. Meet your neighbours in the roadway. Dance ! Sing ! Give thanks and rejoice for your wide gardens and your open land. But it would be useless, I fear. Nothing short of Bolshevism could shatter that sarcophagus of torpor. They would peer from behind their thick curtains, murmur, " Disgraceful ! " send the maid out with a penny, and return to their high tea.

So I took it out of them in song as we rested by Finsbury Park ; and I handed the song to the stud-merchant, who put a tune to it and sang it as we approached Harringay :

> *On Shepherd's Hill the people stay*
> *Inside their houses all the day.*
> *They never laugh, or sing, or shout,*
> *Or dance, or throw themselves about,*
> *But make November of their May.*
>
> *If they are tempted to be gay,*
> *They think : " What would the neighbours say ? "*
> *And so they lock the tempter out*
> > *On Shepherd's Hill.*
>
> *You never see a child at play*
> *Along this treed and flowered way.*
> *I think some Calvinistic drought*
> *Has dried the spring of childhood out ;*
> *For blasphemous silence broods alway*
> > *On Shepherd's Hill.*

At Harringay the scenery of Green Lanes suffers a change. It becomes a Grand Parade with solid shops and good-looking shoppers. Harringay seems to be mildly prosperous. It stands between the showy and the ignoble. Its note is bright respect-ability, in pleasant contrast to the flat respectability of Hampstead and St. John's Wood. As we saw only babies and women on the Grand Parade, I assumed that the male inhabitants work hard in the city all day. Inspecting their women, I fancied the men to be clerks, senior clerks, chartered accountants, and other types of the small fry of E.C. The women seemed to be the decent little wives of men who worked at work that need not wait on inspiration, ploddingly, and took pride in their homes and gardens, and "put a little bit by."

One thing I like about Harringay, and that is the example in local patriotism that it sets to other suburbs. Half of it belongs to Tottenham, the other half to Hornsey, the boundary line intersecting a dozen short roads of villas. But do you think the inhabitants of those villas will rank themselves with those of Tottenham or Hornsey? Not likely. They are of Harringay. The guide-book was right: it is a suburb with a distinct individuality of its own. Proud of its lineage, proud of its appearance in thirteenth-century records, it declines to surrender its identity to those who claim lordship over it. Before Tottenham and Hornsey were, Harringay was so often mentioned in ancient documents as to receive the honour of being spelt in six different ways—sure proof of importance. Indeed, the name Hornsey came into currency only through a corruption of Haringhea and Haringey; and it is therefore fit that the stout fellows of Harringay should defend the style and identity of their venerable villa.e from the encroachments of that modern upstart Hornsey. At Harringay, where is now Finsbury Park, stood that Hornsey Wood House, famous in the early nineteenth century as a kind of rustic Cremorne. George Crabbe once spent the night in its grounds with a copy of *Tibullus*, being without means of obtaining either a lodging for the night or a coach back to town. Its eel pies were good and cheap, inducements which would lure any poet to the house and lure his last coins from his pocket. At Harringay, too, Gloucester was met by the Lord Mayor of London on his entry into the city with the little Edward, whom he had even then arranged to murder in the Tower ; and in Hornsey churchyard lies Samuel Rogers. That is all I know of the past story of the district. I wonder whether the Harringans, with all their fervour for the perpetuation of their name, know more.

" Throughout these northern suburbs," said I to my companion, as we passed West Green, " the thrill of history falls upon you ——" but the sentence was never finished. He snapped off its tail with a roar :

> *Whow !*
> *When first I went to Harringay,*
> *To Harringay did go,*
> *Sing wo, my lads, sing wo !*
> *I met a maid upon my way,*
> *Towards the hush-time of the day,*
> *When thrushes sang in Harringay :*
> *Sing wo, my lads, sing wo !*

My heart now lies at Harringay
Beneath the Autumn leaves,
    Sing willow, lads, sing willow !
With lure of lip and glances gay
That maid she led my heart away ;
She buried it at Harringay ;
    Sing willow, lads, sing willow !

" Where on earth did you get that ? " I asked.
" That's not one of yours."

" 'Tis," he snapped. " I made it up coming
along." I must have registered incredulity, for he
bit at me with " Awright. Don't believe me if
ych don't want to. But if you know as much as
I do about folksongs and the semteenth-century
song-books, you'd know it's easy to make up things
like that. Easy. I s'pose you think, 'cos I don't
talk grammar and got a Cockney accent, I don't
know much. That's where you're wrong, me boy.
I dessay I'm as well up in the semteenth century
poets as what you are. I was alwis reading 'em
out there, 'cos they're quiet-like. They ain't so full
of glory and liberty, and patriotism, as the others.
They 'ad more sense. That's why I stuck to 'em.
I can give you orf 'and 'alf-a-dozen of George
'Erbert's this very minute. *And* Campion. *And*
Carew. *And* Suckling. Shakespeare I *ain't* read,
I confess. But you can't teach me nothing about
old Inglish songs. So I tell ych. I come across
some of 'em yers ago in a old *Leisure Hour.* And
I bin studyin em ever since.

I soothed his ruffled feelings, not by apology, but by violent argument. I sneered at the seventeenth century, and quoted a stanza of Sedley's "Fair Chloris" as rubbish. Twinkling with delight, he opposed me, and snapped me up for a misquotation. Then, setting his case on the kerb of Green Lanes, he opened it ; and, from the miscellany of studs, scarf-pins, trouser buttons, bootlaces, brooches, bracelets, and cuff-links, he dug out a dowdy copy of an anthology of *Cavalier Lyrics* in the little Canterbury series, and planted a grimed finger on the stanza I had mis-mouthed.

"Now, me boy, you quote him prop'ly, and see if he's poitry or not."

He was happy again. I appealed for an armistice, and we stood shoulder to shoulder above his open shop, turning the pages, recalling familiar lines, interrupting one another with "Yes, but, d'you know Campion's 'There is a garden.'" . . . "Ah, but there's a better one than that—Randolph's 'Come, spur away.' Know it ? And there's old John Donne—'e's 'ere, too. Lovely things" ; until I became aware of a gentle voice at my elbow.

"How much ? How much, please ? "

I turned, and saw a nice old lady with a nice old dog.

"I beg pardon ? " I faltered.

"How much are your bootlaces ? "

Cavalier Lyrics was thrown into my arms, and I was pushed aside.

"Bootlaces, lady? I 'ave 'ere several lines in bootlaces, lady. I on'y carry the best. I 'ave 'ere a very stout pair. Real mohair. Last a year they will, lady. An' on'y eightpence the pair. Try 'em, lady. Finger 'em. Try to snap 'em."

"Er—haven't you anything a little cheaper?"

"Cheaper? Cheaper? Now lemme see. Ah, 'ere's a cheaper line. Not mohair, but strong. Strong. Sixpence they are. The rise in the cost of raw materials, lady . . . you'd 'ardly believe. What with transport as it is, and ——"

"Thank you. I'll take those."

"Thank you, lady. . . . And a nice little favour for the dog? Nice dog, lady. I always 'ad a fancy for Aberdeens meself. This little bit of amber material, now—make a lovely neck ribbon for 'im. I could put that in at tenpence. Oddment, I admit, but that on'y means you can't duplicate it anywhere. Unique. Much obliged. . . . One-and-four altogether. One-and-six—one-and-four—twopence change."

The lady and the Aberdeen trotted away, and he snapped the case close with a joyous click. "Good old semteenth century. If we 'adn't 'ad that row, I'd 'a missed that bit o' business. . . . An' now, what about eatin'? D'you take nourishment this time o' day?'

8

"I can eat eggs and bacon at any time of day or night," I said. "But they don't seem to eat publicly at Harringay. Can you perceive through the eye or the nostrils any manifestation of the existence of the *table d'hôte*, the One-and-sixpenny Ordinary, or the Good Pull Up For Carmen?"

His little eyes flashed from point to point. "Looks like a wash-out," he sighed. "What's that, though —over there?" He pointed down a side street to a little corner public-house. "They got something stuck in the window."

We went to it, and in its small window was an almost illegible but promising menu, and I deciphered sauté potatoes, to which I am always inclined. The odour of liver-and-bacon and fried potatoes and stewed steak hovered about its doorway. We entered the tiny saloon bar, and took a seat at one of two long tables, and ordered. Above the clangour of knives and forks and beer engines and cash-registers rose the voices of the waitresses and the landlady at the kitchen lift.

"Now, Bessie, liver-bacon-'n-sooty potatoes. That yours?"

"No, mum. I had mashed with my one."

"'Ere, Evelyn, 'ere's your boiled leg. D' you 'ave suet with it?"

"No, mum. I got baked and sprouts on that."

"Below, there. . . . Suet coming back. Make it

baked and sprouts.   Bessie, you got a rabbit following
your liver ? "

"Well, well," said my Autolycus, as we sat at
meat, "I'm glad you brought me to 'Arringay.
'Cos I never bin to 'Arringay, an' I love going to
new places.   D'you think I can get a picture postcard
of 'Arringay anywhere ?   I'd like one to show the
missus when I get 'ome where I bin.   Or a bit of
'Arringay rock, or coat-of-arms china, like.   Eh ? "

Truly a fellow of my own shape.

"Yerce, I love going about.   Going into shops,
too.   Any shops.   Oil shops and penny bazaars
specially.   Ever 'eard the ole song about oil-shops ?
I 'eard it sung at a panto., when I was about so
'igh.   'Ow did it go ?

> Black lead and clothes-lines,
> Treacle, peas, and British wines,
> Colours mixed for painting,
> Pots and brushes lent.
> Soap, starch and candles,
> Flanders-brick and turpentine,
> Pepper, glue, and mustard
> Colza oil and scent."

Upon which we left the table, and made for
Wood Green.

WOOD GREEN

THE beauties of Wood Green are not to be taken in a random eyeful. Rather, a loving search must be made for them. The careless, bringing nothing, will bear nothing away. Entering from Green Lanes, your first impression, at that end of the borough, is of sad efficiency. There is an air of tarnished newness about it that depresses you. It seems raw, and a little blown upon. There are no flies on Wood Green in the figurative sense, but at the corner by the Wellington one feels that the flies of North London have often gathered there. Here, too, are open spaces, but spaces that just miss the effect of spaciousness. One feels that these are just building plots that have failed to attract a purchaser. There are decrepit corner lots, shaven of grass, that seem like open wounds. In the April sunshine the red brickwork of the place smote our eyes. Here and there are allotments; and I know of nothing that more quickly suggests squalor and dismay than a few acres of allotments.

As we stood there, I think we both felt contaminated. Dolour gathered about us. Then, a yard or so from our ears, a street organ exploded in a tremolo ragtime, and the whole place became alight and alive for us. With a shake of the feet we turned our backs on the allotments and faced the Grand Parade.

There we found colour, gesture, and brisk back-chat between shopmen and customers. When we saw ahead of us the Wood Green Empire and a large Lyons' tea-shop, we knew that our first cut of the place had been on the underdone side. We knew too that we were on the Northern Heights. Wood Green is a place for breezy " views " ; and, like all airy places, it has been discovered by the philanthropic—not the improving kind; the good-natured kind—and here are Fishmongers' Almshouses, Printers' Almshouses, and Watch and Clockmakers' Almshouses. Oh—there's the Home and Colonial Training College, too. We had not time to inspect this last, and I fancy we must have missed much entertainment. It must be exciting to see eager young apprentices receiving instruction in the craft of slapping butter and margarine into pounds and half-pounds, slicing cheeses, and reaching down the Oolong, the Bohea, and the Pekoe. Its philanthropy is not limited to the exercise of kindness by organized societies. You have but to ask the way to such-and-such a place to discover how ready the natives are to help.

With philanthropy it sorts patriotism. It has its Gladstone Avenue, and its Lovatt Grove, but these pious memorials of ponderous ability are immediately relieved by a Moselle Avenue and a Jolly Butchers' Hill. This latter is good, though in no social history can I find any evidence that butchers were ever jolly. To-day the term is so inept, that the authorities might as well pair it with a Happy Taxi-driver's Crescent. The Town Hall Gardens, with bandstand, are bright and orderly; there are the Nightingale Gardens, where dancing may be had on light evenings; and there is the original Wood Green itself. Nor is this all: there are other oddments of pleasure spaces. The High Road feeds the eye at frequent intervals with these snacks of municipal green.

Wood Green is one of the few London suburbs that lack recorded history. Pepys never saw it. Queen Elizabeth did not sleep here. Sir Walter Besant is silent about it. It is off the main North Road, and has no old taverns or churches. No famous men were born there. I find no word of it in literature. It has been ignored by the novelist, the essayist, and the topographist. There is no Official Guide to its "places of interest." It lives wholly in its golden and romantic present. Its people seem to be full-blooded, with appetite for adventure; for the L.G.O.C. find it pays to run 'buses from Wood Green, N., to Shooter's Hill and Sidcup, Kent, every day. You should see the natives on warm Saturdays and Sundays, in their "best things," with Johnny and Marjorie and Hyacinth and Maudie,

in *their* " best things," how they cluster about these
'buses, and clamber with many noises to the top.
They surely know how to go on a journey. I am
no miser of my emotional processes ; my strings
are always taut and eager to speak, to the lightest
caress. But never, I am sure, could I achieve the
vociferous delight that these good matrons and dads
wrest from their ride across London to the edge of
Kent. If fresh delight in simple things is the heritage
of the happy man, then Wood Green glitters with
joy. They have an enormous capacity for surprise.
To these darlings the day's things are ever new,
ever affording novel aspects, wrapped in an inex-
haustible sheath of gowns. Such joy is never to
be found with the stupefied rustic or the highly-
educated urban. It belongs to those who fall between
the two : to those who can express emotion and have
not yet learnt that to express emotion is indecent.
Every noise they make is a thanksgiving for good
things ; and they are prodigal of thanks. So do
they get many good things and much joy ; while
the occupants of " substantial " villas, knowing not
how to praise, are left to eat their own peevishness.
Man lives by that exquisite sense of proportion
which we call humour, and that sense is most largely
found among the impecunious. Authors, artists, and
dramatists, presenting humour, have always gone
for their material to the unlearned and the rude—
for these are alive. No great comedy or work of

humour has been set among the well-bred and the
elegant, for these are afraid to be natural; they can
only be vulgar in the worst sense of that word.

The simple toiler from the factory bench will see
more and gather more in a half-hour's 'bus ride
than some can gather in a trip round the world. A
poster, a bizarre frock, a strange building, a factory,
a bicycle accident, the deportment of pedestrians—
all come to them with the shock of a novel vaudeville
turn. Deep Homeric laughter is aroused by an old
man who takes a walk without a hat. The wells
of wit are tickled when a fat one scurries from the
path of the 'bus. They talk with large accents.
They cry aloud. They are spendthrift of expression.
Oh, they do so enjoy it all! How they contrive to
preserve such appetite for enjoyment from the
clutching hands of factory, office, and back-kitchen,
is a question that no Fabian pamphleteer has yet
answered. I will not try to answer it; for such
researches I have no mind. It is enough that it is
there. I am content to accept the fact of their
rejoicing, since joy expressed is everybody's joy.

I wonder whether the folk who live in the costly
mansions of Shooter's Hill ever take the 'bus ride
to Wood Green; and, if so, whether they go to Wood
Green as gladly as Wood Green goes to Shooter's
Hill. I doubt. I think I know my Shooter's Hill
public. I think I hear them say: "Wood Green?
Where the hell's that?"—if a man—or, if a woman:

" Wood Green ? Wood *Green* ? Oh, isn't that one of those North London slums ? "

Yet they might have great good of a visit to Wood Green. I told you that beauty was to be found in Wood Green, if one sought with the right heart. I will discover it to you.

At Wood Green is the factory of Messrs. Barratt & Co , wholesale confectioners.

That alone gives Wood Green a seal brighter and bolder than that borne by any other suburb. Barratt & Co. are to Wood Green what Shakespeare is to Stratford, Johnson to Lichfield, Mrs. Gaskell to Knutsford, Coleridge to Highgate. I will not say that they are not even an ornament brighter than these. These others have given little joy to children ; but when one thinks of the thousands of dingy shop-windows in dingy by-streets of London that are made lovely by the wares of the Barratt family, so that they become very heavens to the starving eyes of little girls and boys, the stupendous vision of beauty that Wood Green has given to the metropolis leaves one breathless.

Well I remember the little sweetstuff shop where I could lay out my weekly penny in farthing's-worths of the wares of the Barratts. Sumptuously stocked was its window with coloured delights in neat wooden boxes, the inside of the lids blazing with "Barratt & Co , Wood Green, London," in multi-hued lettering. There one would linger for perhaps half-an-hour, discussing with a friend whether Barratt was at his best in his "all-sorts" at four ounces the penny, or whether his "clove-sticks" at a halfpenny each might not prove the more enduring. So, when I came this day to Wood Green, I brought with me my childhood fancy, which was a visualization of Wood Green as one vast sweetstuff shop, where clever men in large white aprons worked among miles of barley-sugar, leagues of clove-stick, acres of cocoa-nut toffee and almond-rock, and mountains of all-sorts; while Barratt & Co.—I always fancied Barratt to be big and bearded and heavily facetious, like one's best uncle, and Co. as a little fellow, spry and tricky, and up to his larks—while Barratt & Co. did nothing but taste their own sweets and order other men about.

Wherefore Wood Green should be a shrine, the goal of a sweet pilgrimage. I would like to see, on May Day, all the children of London, rich and poor, well-dressed and ill-dressed, clean and dirty, parade from slum and suburb to Wood Green, and there do homage to all the Barratts, and assure them prettily of a continuance of esteemed custom. I would not have them garbed for the occasion. They should go in their daily habiliments, boy and girl, boy and girl, two by two, a riot of colour and patches, and lace and rags, as a tactful tribute to the Barratt's "all-sorts." And I would like the little girls to carry posies of London flowers and foliage to lay at the feet of the heroes, while the little boys stood by and cheered. Later in the year there should be a gathering at the Grand Parade of London grown-ups who are still young enough to remember their first suck at a Barratt sweet. I don't suppose they would want to carry posies ; but perhaps the gentlemen could have a whip-round and buy the Barratts a case of pre-war whisky ; and perhaps the ladies could knit them something against the time when the evenings begin to draw in.

As the pedlar and I sat in the Jolly Butchers, I made a lame song as my own contribution, which he put to a tune and with many a clearing of throat, writhing of the lips, and half-arm flourish, sang aloud against much protest from the barmaids :

> *I think I will go to Wood Green*
> *Where the toffee-apples grow,*
> *And in the darkling green wood*
> *See the pear-drops glow.*
> *I will build a house of almond-rock,*
> *And fence it all around*
> *With stout sticks of barley sugar*
> *Planted in the ground.*
>
> *I will bore for a spring of mineral water*
> *Warranted to contain*
> *No " deleterious matter "*
> *To bring a morning pain.*
> *I will have a floor of chocolate bars*
> *And a Turkish delight settee ;*
> *And Barratt shall put me to bed at night,*
> *And Co. shall ut r m.*

I forgot to include among the features of Wood Green a large, four-square building of the type described as " places of amusement." It is called Alexandra Palace. It looks like it. It doesn't amuse me.

BOWES PARK TO ENFIELD

BUT noon was well behind, and we had still half our journey to accomplish. We threw a leg, therefore, northwards, and I walked joyfully; for, in Victoria Station Yard, I had noticed, on fine mornings, when my destination was the office, fleets of motor-buses that were labelled " The Cherry Tree." Often had I longed to be the driver of a bus that went to the Cherry Tree on such mornings. How his heart must sing, as he throws the power on! How he must snort, as he leaves the yard and blusters through the crowds of luckless fellows who are going to work! Were I the driver, I would hark back to the methods of the old horse-drawn affairs, and I would chortle and chi-ike. Thus: "Now, any more for the Cherry TREE! Eightpence all the way! All the way to the Cherry TREE! Now— Cherrin Craws—Oxfer Street—Tonnumcaw Ro'— Kemden—Negsed—Finsbry Pawk—Woogreen an' Cherry TREE! Come along fer the Cherry TREE! All in bloom to-day, lidies! Now's the time for the Cherry TREE! Too late nex' week, gels! The Cherry TREE!" And then I would burst into song:

Come follow, follow me!
Whither shall I follow, follow thee?
To the Cherry, to the Cherry.
To the Southgate Cherry Tree.

With the excitement of making a first journey to
the Cherry Tree, I suffered, too, the excitement that
is always born in me when on the Northern Heights :
the excitement of being at once on the edge of
London and the beginning of England. The fringe
of South London provides no such thrill. You
know too well what is before you : a few abrupt
roads—the Hastings Road, the Dover Road, the
Brighton Road—whose empty miles bring you to
the coast. These south-eastern counties are but a
landing-stage for England, which properly begins at
London. On these northern fringes you may in
fancy face a prospect of illimitable travel. Open,
flowered fields break the loose ranks of shop and
villa, outposts of the rich scenes that lie before you
on these noble ways to a hundred noble cities.

Bowes Park is Wood Green with its Sunday clothes
on. Wood Green is the original Jack Jones ; Bowes
Park is Jack Jones " come into a little bit o' splosh."
The exuberant vulgarity is here chidden and toned
down. Philanthropy and clamorous trade are con-
trolled. Almshouses are not seen, and shops are
few. It is what is called a residential district.
Pride is in the air here ; not an over-blown, pigeon-
breasted, tilt-nosed pride, but the sedate pride of
the humble, of those who will make the best of
themselves and their possessions, while knowing them
to be not of prime quality. The little front gardens
are neatly kept ; the little door-steps and door-

handles gleam and glisten ; the little wives push
little perambulators with nice economy of energy.
People do not to-day keep servants in Bowes Park,
and they look very happy.   I am sure they did keep
servants in the easier days ; not one of those villas
then without "the maid." But now she never
bothers them ; they smile and go gladly about their
work with their own hands on the happy-go-lucky
principle.   Mistresses and young daughters may be
seen every morning cleaning their own steps, performing their own chores.   The weekly turn-out is
a defunct institution.   The drawing-room is no longer
a drawing-room ; it is an untidy room where one
can be at ease.   If you call in the afternoon, you
may be kept waiting at the door until madame has
made her toilet and can decently appear.   And a
happy chorus rises from a thousand tea-tables :
' 'My dear, we simply can't find a servant for love
or money."

And in Bowes Park, as in all suburbs, they are
glad, yea, glad with all their hearts, though they
dare not yet give voice.   For they never really
wanted a servant, and they never could afford a
servant.   They had to have a servant.   It was a
case of hypnotism, of "keeping up with the
Joneses."   In my own suburb my establishment
was for many years unique and discreditable ; it
was the only house in Laburnum Avenue that had
no "maid." Being thus outside the pale, I heard

and saw more of this servant question than those
within it. I was told things that were not told
to others. When Mrs. Delatouche engaged an extra
maid, and thus had a staff of two, I alone knew
the anguished searching of pass-books and the family
committees of ways and means that disturbed other
houses in the Avenue, as they sought to show Mrs.
Delatouche that she was no better than other
Laburnumites. Wherefore all are now joyful. They
look each other in the face. " Had any luck yet ? "
" No. I advertised last week, and offered thirty
pounds a year, and two evenings a week, but not
one reply." And the two liars part with smiles,
knowing that the collapse of the servant market
protects them from discovery. At last the hard-up
professional man has a socially legitimate excuse
for not burdening his home with the Unwelcome
Stranger. His wife can soil her hands and feel
that she is not losing caste. The atmosphere of the
house is brighter, the tone clearer. The maid in the
seven-room villa was always an excrescence. Hus-
band and wife could never discuss private affairs
without lowering their voices. One could never
leave letters and private papers lying about ; one
was always half-aware of the concealed presence of
the Unwelcome Stranger. To-day Mr. Laburnum is
master of his own house, and is discovering the
physical joy and mental stimulation provided by
boot-cleaning and brass-polishing. He feels, as

the Pilgrim felt, when the load fell from his shoulders.

Bowes Park seems to be the work of one builder. He has builded well, but, as he was making a town, he would have done better to have expunged the rural touches and worked for candid urban effects. In two hundred yards of High Road you pass Woodside Road, Sylvan Villas, Arcadian Gardens, and Glendale Avenue. This, I suppose, is meant to bring the happy country tone to the ears of youth and maid, and lead them there to nest ; but as all these roads lead into Wolves' Lane I think any mating couple would show a preference for urban security over this hazardous Arcady.

At Bowes Park, Green Lanes becomes once more Green Lanes until it reaches Palmer's Green, where it becomes a High Road. If Bowes Park is Wood Green in its Sunday clothes, Palmer's Green is a Bowes Park that has " got on." Large villas here, desirable and commodious, with garages and carriage sweeps. Dignified shops, with much glass frontage, in wide streets. The air seems clean and cool and still. One might be in a vast dairy. The tourist who arrives on foot from the cottage gentilities of Wood Green pauses as he takes his first breath of Palmer's Green. There is an austere flavour about it : a fine serenity, almost serendipity. In its streets one becomes chastened, yet not humiliated. No little half-hearted shops here. No penny bazaars

for my friend to "poke about in." No tupp'ny-
hap'ny haberdashers. No combined one-man business of newsagent, tobacconist, confectioner and
barber. No barbers at all—hairdressers only. No
drapery stores or baby-linen shops; but veiled,
contemplative establishments, with empty windows,
labelled Odette or Julie or Yvonne—ladies whose
presence in a suburb is a cachet of social rightness.
Folk don't let themselves go in Palmer's Green.
The word "jolly" is never used; its synonym is
"charming" or "delightful." Children on scooters
proceed along its pavement with almost Chinese
placidity. Everybody proceeds. Even the butchers'
carts proceed. We pilgrims found that the stride
that had brought us thither dropped involuntarily
to a minuet step; and by this step we proceeded
off our route to see the Cherry Tree at
Southgate.

Yet Palmer's Green is not moribund as is Shepherd's
Hill. People do enjoy themselves here. They do
not wear masks; you may share their tranquil pleasure
in things. They can afford comfortably to keep
servants here, and they do keep servants; hence
that institution as well known to the railwaymen of
this line as the Flying Scotchman, or the Cornishman,
or the Brighton Belle : I mean the Dripping Special.
My friend had sold a stud to a porter by the station,
and we fell to chatting about the district and its
notable charms, and about his work. Sunday was

a good day ; he was only on for the Dripping Special ;
when he got that away he was done.

"Dripping Special ?   Oh, that's the three-thirty
up.   The cooks' train. . . .   Eh ?   Oh, I thought
you knew.   Old Ernie give it that name.   All the
domestics from the big 'ouses catch that one fer
town on their Sundays off ; and they all carry parcels.
You know, little tit-bits to take 'ome to their people.
Left-overs from the kitchen and the pantry.   Well,
you know what a godsend a good bit of beef dripping
is to a family of boys and gels, don't yeh ?   Well,
from the smell on that platform before the three-
thirty comes up, they mostly seems to go in fer
dripping.   And good judges, too.   So Old Ernie 'e's
named it 'The Dripping Special '"

From dripping we turned our minds again to the
Cherry Tree.   You come to it by Alderman's Hill
(this must be Jolly Butchers' Hill risen to civic
honours), which borders a large natural public park,
with rich turf and a round pond girdled by patrician
elms.   Children play here—in a gentlemanly way,
of course.   Our day was well chosen.   Some weeks
of sun and shower had loaded the front gardens
with the opulent bloom of rhododendron, lilac,
laburnum, chestnut, red and white hawthorn, wistaria,
and the smouldering hue of copper beeches.   A few
wooden   thatched   cottages   were   everywhere
shouldered and bunted by the villas of 1914, and
did not seem to know what to make of it.   South-

gate itself seems uncertain whether to be a village, or to admit the intruders and be a thriving and up-to-date suburb. It seems to meet the intruders without welcome and without hostility. " Well," it seems to say, " you've got here, and you came quietly and orderly; so we suppose you'd better stay. The laws of hospitality forbid our refusing you, after so long a journey. But please understand that we cannot recognize or entertain you. You must be self-supporting, and you must keep yourselves decently in the outer courtyard. We don't like the look of you. On the other hand, your behaviour does not warrant us in packing you about your business. So, if you continue in quiet conduct, you can stay or go, as you please."

The Cherry Tree faces the village green, and stands modestly back from the road, as a village inn should. Its architecture is unremarkable. It was apparently built on the site of a more picturesque predecessor. But certainly it is an inn, and not a public-house Your nose tells you that when you enter, for the bar exudes the rich country smell that never can be counterfeited. It is drawn from the wood that has been seasoned by decades of smoke and human rubbings and the outdoor perfumes of years. It seems to be compounded of the kindly spirits of the past, as a promise of good company and entertainment. No London bar, however ripe in years, can produce that odour of welcome ; its

patrons are too numerous and too often scattered
to make a club or coterie. The appointments of
the Cherry Tree catch happily the tact of its atmosphere. There are a few Rowlandson prints ; some
pieces of old pewter ; a long, low billiard room,
coaching pictures, and sturdy tables and elbow
chairs. From the curtained window one looks across
the green, and down the road whither go the 'buses
to Chase Side.   And from the back you see Alexandra
Palace. It is impossible to escape Alexandra Palace
in North London, or even in Middlesex, Hertfordshire or Essex. But there is happily little local
pride in it. The folk at Muswell Hill are much
more fluttered to show you the view of the Crystal
Palace from their " Green Man " on a clear day ;
even as those of South London are loud upon their
view of Harrow Spire when atmospheric conditions
are favourable.

It didn't take my friend long to sell a card of
studs and two tie-clips. This was done in one
minute. Then, having praised the landlady's beer
and congratulated her on the lovely country she
had round these parts, he presented her with a little
sachet of lavender, and stood twinkling upon the
three or four customers.

" I *am* glad I come," he chortled into his tankard.
" Fresh air, exercise, an' good beer. What more
can yeh want ? I always say, give everybody
plenty to eat and plenty of good beer to drink,

and you'll never 'ear the word revolution. You'll
never even 'ave discontent. There ain't a revolution what ever 'appened in 'istory but what began
in man's stomach. Take away the franchise an' all
that political stuff, but, as long as they leave us good
food an' drink, we'll be 'appy. . . . Can't somebody
sing a song ? "

" We're not allowed to have any disturbance,"
said the lady.

" All right, mum. We'll sing very soft and low.
Just 'um, y' know. . . . But ain't it awful that you
can't even sing a song but what they calls it creating
a disturbance? . . . Can't you 'um a song, sir ? "

The little old man to whom he turned looked up
and gave back his twinkle.

"I useter knaw a soang once."

"Lessave it then. 'Ow did it go ? "

" I dunnoa. Summin laike this." And he produced in a husky quaver :

> Ol' Jawn 'ad an apple tree 'ailthy an' green
> That bore the best apples that aiver was seen. . . .

" Noa, that i'n' it. 'Ow'd it go ? I knaw :

> Cold's the wind, and wet's the rain,
> Saint Hugh be our good speed ;
> Ill's the weather that brings no gain,
> Nor helps good hearts in need.

> Troll the bowl, the jolly nut-brown bowl,
> And here's, kind mate, to thee ;
> Let's sing a dirge for Saint Hugh's soul,
> And down it merrily.

"Damgood song," said Studdy. "Can't no one else do nothing ?"

"Here you are," I said, "you can hum this. You hum much better than I can." And I handed him a spent envelope from which he rather more than hummed these lines suggested by the last few miles of our tramp :

> *Wood Green's a little woman*
> *Who leads a woman's life ;*
> *A careful, candid mother,*
> *A busy, cheerful wife.*
> *But Palmer's Green's a lady*
> *Who rises after nine,*
> *The Woodgreens have their dinner,*
> *But the Palmer-Greeners dine.*
>
> *Now Southgate's like a young maid*
> *Who does not know her mind,*
> *But harks to every message*
> *That's borne on every wind.*
> *When Town and Country wooed her,*
> *From each she turned her eyes,*
> *And now she's settled down in dull*
> *And horrid compromise.*
>
> *Bowes Park has just got married ;*
> *The orange blossom shows*
> *Upon her . . . .*

The sonorous voice, "Now time, gentlemen, please !" and the general disturbance of the company broke the song into fragments. Studdy gathered up his case of merchandise, and we turned back to Palmer's Green, where we should again pick up Green Lanes. We were now tired, and boarded a car which waited by the old thatched and mullioned cottage, dated 1795, now used as a coal order office. Have you, if your wanderings occasion you to long 'bus and tram routes, noticed the fine improvement in the conductor's manners, as his car or 'bus gets farther from the bricks ?   At these outer districts they become human.   They are as they should be ; as Charles Keene and Phil May created them.   They are prodigally polite.   They make jokes.   The fresh breeze inspires them to be mildly flirtatious with young girls and very kindly towards old ladies with baskets.   They whistle a stave or so.   They keep the car waiting, if signalled from side streets.   The car we boarded was empty on top, so, before going up, I handed our fares to the conductor to save him a needless trip.   He said : " Thank you very much, sir.   Very considerate of you."   The same man at Camden Town would have snapped, " Thanks ! "   At Tottenham Court Road he would not have done that.

At Winchmore Hill, Green Lanes breaks from the dusty shackles of town and roams into the open. Here it is bordered by fields of flowers amid which that day stood children breast-high.   I thought of Birket Foster's country pictures, and spoke to Studdy of them.   (I was then calling him Studdy.)   He did not know them ; but he did know Henry Vaughan's— " I walked the other day, to spend my hour, into a field . . ." and quoted it.   I was glad we were alone on the car. Had we been accompanied he would have tried to sell studs, and Henry Vaughan and traffic in studs might have seemed a little incongruous to others. We might have attracted remark.

The forms of worship in the Winchmore Hill district seem to be those of the Corrugated Baptists. At every turn and bend are little tin temples, each seating with comfort, I reckon, twenty-five grown people. Small and select, I suppose, in worship as in social life.

And so to Enfield, where Green Lanes loses its identity for ever. It was dusk when we arrived, and I was glad. Pepys came to Enfield at dusk. One should always come to old towns at dusk, and seek with tired legs the lighted inn in the High Street. Rain had fallen before we came, and the sombre line of pavement was interrupted by radiant smears. Against the subdued lights of the principal inn the old church tower loomed as a pillar of cloud rather than substance. Its gates are separated by some three feet from the door of the inn parlour, towards which Studdy led the way. Enfield is soaked in historic association; yet this church is most all that survives of its grand days. Oh, there is a butcher's shop kept by one Charles Lamb. Whether this be his true name, I know not; nor, if it be adopted, whether he took it as a heavy jest upon his profession or in celebration of one already associated with Lon—hl   The sight of that name and that shop, however, recalled to me a passage that I have always carried in a corner of memory :

" Then, do you remember our pleasant walks to Enfield . . . when we had a holiday—holidays and all other fun are gone now we are rich—and the little hand-basket in which I used to deposit our day's fare of savoury cold lamb and salad—and how you would pry about at noon-tide for some decent house, where we might go in and produce our store, only paying for the ale that you must call for, and speculate upon the looks of the landlady and whether she was likely to allow us a table-cloth—and wish for such another honest hostess as Izaak Walton has described many a one on the pleasant banks of the Lea."

Yes, there is much to be said for Pelmanism if it enables you to call up at the time and the place such passages as that.   The doings in Enfield of Elizabeth, James I, and the Gunpowder Plotters lose their savour when served with the sharp sauce of that prose.   It came as a pleasant night-cap to our day. I had found the end of Green Lanes.   I hurried home to find my battered pocket edition of Elia.

HACKNEY

" With my wife only to take the ayre, it being very warm
and pleasant, to Bowe ; and thence to Hackney. There
light and played at shuffle-board, eat cream and good cherries ;
and so with good refreshment home."

THUS Master Samuel Pepys, on June 11, 1663.
To-day his cherry gardens are the Metropolitan Borough of Hackney, with a population of a quarter of a million. Yet it does not
give itself airs. It carries itself with decent, if
somewhat stodgy dignity. When you stand in
Mare Street, you know that you are in a borough,
but there is nothing of the grandiose about it.
Rather, it diffuses an aura of comfort, of the physical
well-being attending upon an aldermanic feast.

It was a June day when I went to Hackney to
take the ayre and see the sights, some two hundred
and sixty years after Pepys ; but there was no
cream to be had, and cherries were two shillings
the pound. Nor could I get a game of shuffle-board
—probably an early form of shove-ha'p'ny ; though
I prefer the term " shuffle-board," as I prefer the term
" stool-ball " to " cricket."

A young gentleman in leggings, whom I met in a

house of public entertainment, offered me, in a husky voice, a hundred up ; but I don't play billiards, and I declined. He then suggested that I should tell him in which hand the button was, at a bob a time, " for a bit o' sport, like." I wonder why those who wear spectacles are always taken as soft marks for proposals of this sort ; and I wonder whether Pepys, on his visit to Hackney, was accosted by this young man's great-great-great-great blood relation.

Nor can I write—" with good refreshment home." Hackney is shy of the visitor. There is no place at the board for him, either above or below the salt. A fly-blown Italian restaurant, with an odour of the week before last, forms its single gesture of welcome to the wayfarer. True, it has many taverns, but none of them makes any attempt to rescue, from the decay into which it is falling, that charming institution—the daily " ordinary."

In other respects, it is what is known as a progressive suburb. It has an " Empire," and is rich (as my school geography used to say)—rich in picture palaces. It must not be inferred from this that all the people of Hackney are of enfeebled intellects. Oh, no ; it is only a minor section of the inhabitants that finds entertainment in this mechanical, jig-saw, penny-in-the-slottery, cheap-gaff shadow trickery.

You will infer from this that I dislike the cinema. I loathe the cinema. I loathe it because I loathe

anything that pretends to be what it is not. Most
inventions and enterprises show, in twenty years, a
forward movement ; but after twenty years the
cinema is still where it was. After twenty years of
life the cinema is still in the street of the penny
gaff. It is still produced by office boys for office
boys. Yet its promoters have the impudence to
speak of it as a new art, and of their aiders and
abettors as artists.

One cannot reasonably object to the penny gaff.
It is quite right that the office boy, and his grown-up
equals, who like their entertainment hot and strong,
should be supplied with what they like. But when
the penny gaff claims for itself dignity and consideration as a new art-form—just because it can
pay its workers enormous salaries—then one is
justified in asking it to get off its perch.

It is time that somebody said what most people
are thinking about this shoddy business of cameras
and clap-trap, and the ill-informed people who direct
it. Consider its "artists." Their "acting" consists
of portentous foolery—facial grimaces and club-footed
antics. Analyse the work of the world's favourite,
Mary Pickford. This lady can simper and smile
very charmingly, but her amiable gestures are utterly
meaningless. Of the delicate art of pantomime she
is entirely ignorant. Her producers and directors
have sufficient brains to recognize this ; so between
her posturings the insert shots of letterpress—

usually hostile to the laws of grammar—to tell you what she is doing.

There is but one among the whole crowd of " movie stars " who has the slimmest understanding of gesture ; and he, unfortunately, who might be doing better things, spends his time capering about in large boots and a misfit bowler hat. One does not need illiterate letterpress to explain what he is doing ; and, if he would throw away his present make-up and come out in " straight " parts, the cinema would possess a pantomimist who would shame all others out of the business.

When one remembers the Russian Ballet and the exquisite *L'Enfant Prodigue,* one is appalled at the work of the simpering people who are boosted as artists. If the picture-play were truly a new art, it would achieve its effects solely through its own medium, and not one word would be necessary to explain the grimaces of the artists. But it is not a new art, and never will be. You cannot tell a story through so blunt and unaccommodating a medium as photography.

Apologists for the cinema have said : " Yes, but it will be better, when serious novelists write stories directly for the screen." I sincerely hope that no serious novelist will do any such thing. The novelist, if he is an artist, achieves his effects by the nice handling of words. The power of words is far greater than the power of pictures, because words *say* less than pictures. Words themselves are nothing : they are hints, murmurings, suggestions. Words have atmosphere, fluency, music, associations which the photograph can never possess. A photograph says everything it has to say, and can suggest nothing more. The most perfect photograph has only the effect on the spectator of a witnessed street accident. The thing is there. You have seen it. Nothing is left to the imagination.

When an author, in the course of a story, throws in a suggestion that a child is ill-treated by its father, an atmosphere is created, and, if the author has suitably conveyed that atmosphere, the reader's imagination is clothed with it, and he is filled with pity by the half-known thing. But when moving pictures are presented to an audience, showing a brutal father whipping his child with a dog-whip, art is left out, and the audience suffers nothing of that pity—only nausea. The thing *seen* (as in the cinema) only shocks or fails to interest ; it is the thing suggested and touched by the magic of words (as in literature) that lifts the miserable to the tragic. A headless body on a battlefield is not a tragic sight : it is a revolting sight. But the phrase— " He died in battle for his country "—does carry something of the beauty and tragedy that inspires the hearer.

But my main objection to the cinema is its effect on the child. It is robbing the child of to-day of the exercise of that most precious faculty—imagination. In the cinema the children, who, appropriately, constitute its most numerous patronage, are shown everything as it is. Not for one moment are they allowed to think or to give rein to their fancy. They are shown foreign countries, foreign people going about their daily tasks, foreign religious ceremonies, and so on, in full activity, and their minds are sent empty away. Words awake imagination; pictures kill it. When I was a child, I could find the map of Asia as enthralling as *Andersen's Fairy Tales* or *Robinson Crusoe*. My school geography had furnished me with rough facts about Far Eastern countries, and I could pore over the map, and build its cities for myself. Certainly I built them all wrong; but how delicious was the process of building, and how valuable was that early training of the imagination !

To-day the child's imagination is stultified at every turn. He is shown everything in its crude and unsatisfying reality. There is no suggestion round which his mind can play. There is no opportunity for wonder. He is given the bare substance and robbed of the delicious enduring shadow. He can correct my wild surmises of Kurdestan and Baluchestan : he has *seen* them. Thanks to the cinema, he will never know the joy of creating them. I can recall how, many years ago, for the mass of the people, a halo of mystery encircled that almost legendary figure, Gladstone ; and veneration lapped the foot of the throne of that remote lady, Victoria. But the child of to-day has seen all the members of the Cabinet that rules him performing their capers on the screen ; and veneration has fled before it.

Many who detest as much as I do the rubbish that is shown in the picture-theatres uphold the cinema as a valuable aid in the school-room for purposes of study. Personally, I would rather it continued in its present money-making game of wheedling ninepences from the office boy, and kept well away from the school-room. Otherwise, in twenty years time there will be an end of Imagination and Fancy ; there will be no more Lantern-Bearers.

Fortunately, it has not yet captured the whole of Hackney. Hackney has still a charming example of Imagination and Fancy in its Parliamentary representative.

From my brief survey of the natives, and from the fact that it is supplied with no fewer than twenty-five Council schools, I put the average of Hackney intelligence at eighty under proof. It is strong on education : it has schools for the deaf, laundry schools, cookery schools, manual training schools, public baths, a disinfecting station, a—in short, everything that is likely to promote material well-being.

Only the finer inwardness of the mind is ignored. Morals receive excessive attention. The Cult of Interferingness flourishes here. The Salvation Army has halls in Havelock Road and Mare Street, and Barracks in Mallard Street ; and the Y.M.C.A. and the Y.W.C.A. busy their bodies, if not their souls, in Mare Street.

Politics, too, are more in Hackney than a mere gambit for conversation. It supports seven or eight political clubs, and takes the preposterous business seriously. Unlike even the least progressive suburbs, it has not, so far as I could discover, a " Literary and Scientific Society," but as Literature has no economic value, one could hardly expect it to appeal to Hackney.

As I have said, its outlook is wholly towards the materialistic. It has an ample and comprehensive history for which it does not give a damn. It shares, with the progressive City Corporation, a careful contempt for non-productive survivals of the past, and has successfully rid itself of all out-of-date architecture.

A few old houses—including Sutton House, where lived old Thomas Sutton, founder of the Charterhouse—remain in the Borough ; but they stand in Clapton and Homerton, not in Hackney proper.

Even its open spaces, of which it possesses nine, seem to be designed more for the welfare of the body than for the stimulation of the mind. The most optimistic of the city fathers could hardly speak of Hackney Downs in connection with calm contemplation and a mind at ase ; and what shall be said of thee, thou foul, flat, dank, dour, noisome, mephitic, miserable Hackney Marsh? Thirty years ago an Earl of Meath described thee as " the most magnificent playground in the world ! " If he were not speaking, as chairmen often do speak, through the back of his neck, then I fear he was pulling thy leg. Mr. Frederick Bingham, from whose *Guide* I have quoted this encomium, admits the utilitarian purpose of these open spaces, but does not apologize.

Springfield Park, which really belongs to Clapton, alone makes any pretension to sylvan and pastoral charm. Here is some little repose, some geniality. Springfield Park is quietly dressed and carries itself well, sharply distinct from the " Gorblimey " deportment of the Downs and the Marshes. Many years ago, Mr. Gus Elen was telling us, in praise of his London garden, that :

> Wiv a pair of op'ry glasses
> You could see to 'Ackney Marshes,
> If it wasn't for the 'ouses in between.

Well, he should have been grateful that there *were* houses in between, to shield him from such an eyesore.

Speaking of 'Ackney, what an exercise in aspirates is afforded by the nomenclature of North London. If only its young natives repeated, every morning before breakfast, the place-names from N.E. to N.W., we should hear less of 'Ackney and 'Igit. South of the river one finds very few " h's ";

they seem to have settled as a family in the north. Here is a round dozen : Hackney, Homerton, Haggerston, Hoxton, Highgate, Hornsey, Hampstead, Harringay, Highbury, Holloway, Harlesden and Hendon. South of the river I know of two—Herne Hill and Hatcham. Perhaps some reader can find another ?

Adjoining Hackney is its obscure, frayed, poor relation, Shacklewell : a queer little district lying lost in a rude triangle formed by Amhurst Road, Dalston Lane and Kingsland High Street. In the sixteenth century Shacklewell was a noble manor, and its Lord married a daughter of Sir Thomas More.

To-day it is formless tract of close streets, with houses neither new nor old. Smudgy decency is its note. It is like a family of ancient lineage that has " gone in " for trade, and has lost its own dignity without acquiring the easy vulgarity of its competitors. It is soaked in self-commiseration ; incapable of self-help. It is without lustre. It might be that Victorian parlour, where certain people sat, " all silent and all damned." Yet its people are not silent, and they do not take their note from their environment. They are happy, and they must be good ; for only very good people could hold happiness amid the unlovely wastes of Shacklewell.

In a small, forlorn " place " in Shacklewell I met —I knew he was somewhere about : he always is— I met the old, old man who minded the time (or should one say *mound* the time ?) when " Shacklewell

an' 'Ackney were all carn-vealds; ey, in them days
there warn't none o' this 'ere." And as I turned
my back on the dolours of Shacklewell and the
clamours of Hackney, and footed it across North
London to the pleasaunces of my own Highgate, I
did this :

When Hackney kept its carriages,
    And in Mare Street mares were found,
There warn't no blasted kinemas,
    And a pound was worth a pound.
The gals *was* gals in them days,
    And beer *were* beer, me boy ;
And pints was pints, and sometimes quarts,
    And 'earts was full of joy.

The fellers then *was* fellers ;
    They didn't try to play
At being something lar-di-dar,
    Like fellers do to-day.
Then it was—" Wodder y'aving, Jarge ? "
    And—" 'Ave this, Jarge, wi' me ! "
But now there ain t no nothing
    Like what it useter be.

WALTHAMSTOW

O N a bright brusque morning a bespoke tailor and another man went by road from Tottenham to Walthamstow.

They met in Lordship Lane, the one buying a morning edition of an evening paper, as the other approached with charming address, desiring to know whether Ice Cream Cornet was regarded with favour for the two o'clock. A few perfunctory remarks followed the satisfaction of this desire, and they moved separately in the same direction ; the yards between them dwindling as they reached the High Road. Here a group of sightseers, inspecting a loaded furniture van with a wheel off, drew them into intimacy. The bespoke tailor remembered a funny story in which a furniture van held a leading part. The other man, stung to competition, remembered one about a green baize apron ; and thereafter they walked about together and agreed in everything.

It fell out that the other man desired to see Walthamstow, so the bespoke tailor, being his own master, was ready to join him and be a guide. He showed no wonder at the business which occasioned

the man to Walthamstow. He walked with him
and discoursed affably of this and that; leading
the way through the Hale, past the old cattle
pound, across the Lea and the Mill-stream, to the
Ferry Boat inn, where Ferry Lane begins. He
pointed out the Refuse Destructor, of which Tottenham is so proud that it gives a full-page plate in
the local guide, with a page and a half of descriptive
letterpress. It is a very fine refuse destructor; a
very stiff, straight, bald destructor; a Hun of a
destructor.

No tram-car awaited them at Ferry Lane, so
a pause at the Ferry Boat inn was suggested. The
Ferry Boat inn is in London. With its rustic porch,
its pinafore of roses, its cascade of creeper, and the
sheets of water that surround it, it entices the villa
residents into the depths of Shropshire. From it
one may look across that broad expanse of water
and marsh that stretches south from Tottenham to
Canning Town, and severs a thick slice of the East
End from the main body of the town. Lucky folk
who live between Tottenham and Walthamstow!

When the Chingford car arrived, the bespoke
tailor and the other man (who was myself) mounted
on top; and my companion produced his patterns
for his new Spring suitings. This was not by way
of advertisement, I am sure; he threw them care-
lessly on my knee and asked me to cast my eye
over them. I said that they looked very good

value, and asked if he had been long in the profession.

" Oh, I bin a cutter for yers. But on'y lately on me own. It's very interesting, y'know, building up a little business. More exciting than backing 'orses, though I 'ave a little on nows and thens, when I 'ear anything reliable. Don't know whether I shall make a Do of it. Sometimes I think I shan't, y'know. I like it, though. It's a nice trade— dressing people up—'specially this time o' year. What I say is : Appearance is everything in the Spring. Ev'body ought to 'ave new suits to go with the Spring sunshine. It makes 'em feel better, and it makes the streets look better and cheers ev'body else up. Dowdy in the winter, if yeh like, but fer Gorsake come out with a bit o' colour in the Spring. I always urge a bit o' colour on all my young customers, and take a pride in turning 'em out, too. Now my gel, Frances, she goes to the extreme. Too many new frocks, and altogether too much colour. I can cut fer ladies, too, but she won't 'ave my tailor-mades. Will go in fer fal-lals and that sort o' thing. As I says to 'er, it's all right fer Lady Diana. Look at the position the gel's got to keep up. But fer our Frances—no. A thousand times—no. Neatness for 'er, as a tailor's daughter. . . . That's Essex Hall down there, that is—down that road. See the top of it. Very old place. Useter be a school. Old Disraeli went to school there. Wouldn't think it, would yeh, to look at it? 'E did, though. That's Lloyd Park what we're coming to, on the left. Very nice. Band plays there in the summer. 'Ere's 'Oe Street. May's well git orf 'ere.''

We got off. I stood in Forest Road and sniffed the atmosphere. My countenance must have registered perplexity, for a civil-spoken gentleman approached us. '' They ain't opening to-day,'' he said oracularly, with a backward jerk of the head. '' Come down in the car? Ah. I can tell y'of a place what will open. Course, I don't tell ev'body. But if any genterman asks me, I'm always willing to give him the information.''

His hand moved before him, opening and closing. We thanked him for his kind offer, but Walthamstow was waiting to uncover her charms to us, and we strolled down Hoe Street. Walthamstow— You probably think of it with a tolerant smile ; and you repeat its syllables—*Walt*hamstow—with an accent of scorn on the first. But as we moved about its streets, touched here and there with tressed trees of laburnum, chestnut, and lilac, I was glad to know Walthamstow.

Walthamstow, I learn from the local guide, has a population of about 150,000, and five railway stations. I had known before that it was the largest of all London's '' dormitories,'' since it was able to demand and obtain an all-night service to and from

Liverpool Street. But I did not know that its municipal reports carried what Defoe has called "such a rumbling sound of great numbers." I did not know about the five railway stations. I did not know a lot of things I learnt in five minutes in the Public Library. Our approach to the place had given me an impression that it had connection with the past; but I had not known that it was so rich in story, or that it was so rich in people. Nowhere else have I seen streets and houses crowd so closely one upon the other. Wave after wave of villas rolls eastward to break upon the green of Essex. Never are its highways at peace; always there is a stir of men returning to rest or rising to labour.

It is well placed. It is airy and open, as a dormitory should be. It has the Lea on its west, the Forest on its east, Chingford on its north, and Leyton on its south. Not content with the Lea, it has produced two minor streams—the Ching and Dagenham Brook. It has a good dozen of Tudor and Georgian mansions and half a dozen High Schools; and significantly substantial Town Hall, Library, and Swimming Bath. These facts I have taken from the Guide to Walthamstow. It is the only guide I know that berates its own subject. Of the Parish Church it says:

"The church is devoid of any architectural or antiquarian pretensions. . . . The interior is not beautiful; the proportions are not good ; and the fittings and furniture are of little interest."

Surely that is unique in guide-book literature.

Of more interest than the church are the houses. In that which is now the lodge of Lloyd Park lived William Morris, and in the moat that surrounds it he swam and boated in his youth. Other great names hang about Walthamstow—Martineau, Cardinal Wiseman, Granville Sharp, Milner Gibson, Morell Mackenzie and Samuel Pepys. Pepys paid many a visit hither ; once to a christening at a Mrs. Browne's, and on the other occasion to the house (now demolished) of Sir William Batten, who kept a vineyard. " He did give the company that were there a bottle or two of his own last year's wine, growing at Walthamstow, than which the whole company said they never drank better foreign wines in their lives." The Monoux Almshouses, of the sixteenth century, are a charm and satisfaction to the eye ; as suave and harmonious as " Cook's Folly " is preposterous.

But what I found most " taking " about Walthamstow were these things : The languid curvature of Hoe Street ; the short, snappy High Street ; the happy architectural mixture of ancient and modern, of proud and paltry ; the American Candy Saloon and Cream-Soda Bar , and the view from Highams across the vast plain of homes.

About Forest Road there is an unseemly decency ;

a down-at-heel-ness of one who has lost both means
and capacity for joy; crazy shops, untenanted
shops, and late Victorian workmen's cottages. But
Hoe Street takes an interest in itself. Its upper
end holds a number of old private houses turned
into shops, such as you see in expanding country
villages. They have stood the change very well.
Instead of bewailing their loss of gentility, they
seem to enter cheerily into the new estate. In the
dining-room window are displayed the goods, and
you mount steps to an august front door which
admits to the counter. Pinched and penurious the
shops and houses are, but by no means dowdy.
They make the best of things. The street is fragrant
of the beauty and simplicity of common people.
Like the unheeded flowers that beautify the waste
places about the town, they are strong, but neither
use nor display their strength ; they are oft trodden
upon, but are seldom crushed and never murmur.
These of Walthamstow know how to enjoy. They
support a dozen picture-palaces. They have half
a dozen recreation grounds. They have, in Hoe
Street, the Victoria Theatre, where good resounding
melodrama shows them the sweetness and light of
their own humble lives and the bitter darkness
that cloaks the heart of Society. They have, in
the High Street, a Gulliver music-hall and an American Ice-Cream Bar. The men are sporty fellows,
for Walthamstow is on the road to Newmarket,

and the breeze from the Heath carries news to Walthamstow. "Information" trips down the road from the stables, and is tripped up and pinioned at Walthamstow, and held to the ransom of those who seek Good Things.

Very ductile the week's wages must become under the hands of the wives of Walthamstow, for they make both ends meet in a wide circle. Their motto seems to be: "We haven't got much money, but we do see life." Certainly they do. They walk jauntily. There is no apathetic bargaining, as in some suburbs, at the butcher's and the fishmonger's. It is bargaining hale and hearty. The parties strip to it and enter in fine tune.

At its southern end Hoe Street improves its exterior. It is preened and polished. The shops are larger and extravagant with plate glass. Here are groups of early Georgian houses, well-preserved and of courtly mien. But the shops are undismayed by their august company; and between two of the groups a green and white and gold picture-palace has squatted. That is a gesture wholly superb; the challenge of youth to age; the irreverent defiance of the immutable. It jostles these stagnant elders, to say: "Pass along, there, now. Pass along, old man. You've made your history. Pass along, and give other people a chance to make theirs."

At the American Ice Cream Bar the bespoke tailor and I paused and admired its aluminium fittings, its bottles of coloured fruit juices, its tinkle of ice and its noise of effervescence. The day was warm. We entered and rested, and ordered a " banana squash " (I think the dish was thus named). It was a tumbler of flavoured soda-water, in which floated ice-cream and a sliced banana. Following the table manners of Mr. Salteena in *The Young Visiters*, we lapped it up thankfully.

" Ha ! " said the tailor, as he set down his glass, " in the words of the poet Champion, ' that was a milky one.' "

" Like it ? " The question came in adenoidal accents from a young Jewess at the next table. She was sucking a long drink through a straw. Her bearing invited talk.

" It was as good as the drink that old Pepys had when he came to Walthamstow."

" Reely ? I like these American drinks. This your dinner hour ? "

" No. We're just having a look round."

" I see. Strangers here. Got a day off from the office, like, and come for a ride on the 'bus, I s'pose ? Bit dull here, ain't it ? I work round here. You know—no Life. I like a bit of life, I do. Wish I could get a job in the City or up West, somewhere. . . . Hullo, Rube."

A staggering suit of clothes entered the bar and sat down at her table. Breathless conversation followed.

The bespoke tailor turned to me. " Artist by any chance ? "

" No," I replied.

" Ha. Thought p'raps you might be, as you seem to got your time to yourself. And yet you ain't as shabby as most artists. I knew a artist once. But so shabby. So dowdy. Bought 'is clothes anywhere—readies—wherever 'e 'appened to be. Come out in all sorts of slops. Reely, I was ashamed to be seen about with 'im sometimes. Me being a tailor, y'know, it looked so bad. . . . Would it be rude of me to enquire what you do ? "

" Oh—I write."

" What—stories and things ? Reely ? Fancy that, now. . . . 'Ere, just look at that chap going out—what's been talking to the gel. Now there's a wicked waste for yeh. Them clothes of 'is must 'a cost 'im a pritty penny. I can tell that by the stuff. But look at the cut. Look at the building. Kind o' thing that makes me angry. I'd chuck up business 'fore I'd turn a lad out like that—or let 'im turn 'isself out like it. Wicked, I call it. But there's 'eaps o' tailors like that—take no interest in their job."

" Ssss ! " The sibilants came from the lady behind us. We turned.

" My brother just gone out."

" Oh ? "

" 'M. He's a awful good boy to me. Awful fond of me."

" Is he ? "

" 'M. Always giving me presents. Look what he's just give me. Blouse-pin. Ain't it lovely ? Have a look at it." She passed it to us. It was not from the local emporium. It was the genuine article, though a little flashy. " Always doing that, he is. Other Sunday he come home with a lovely box of scented soap for me. One-and-ten he give for it. Got it trade price from a friend who's in that line. On'y I wasn't there. I'd gone out to my Aunt Rachel's. So he sold it to my young sister for one-and-two. He wouldn't a' sold it to me, though. He'd 'a give it to me."

The tailor nudged me. " There's a story for yeh," he whispered, with other nudges. " A chap who can write could make a 'ole story out o' that, eh ? "

I nodded. I was making a few notes on Walthamstow.

" Ssss. What's he writing there ? "

" Making notes," replied my friend. " 'E's an author."

" OO. Are you ? Reely ? What you writing about ? "

" I'm writing about Walthamstow now."

" Oo. About us ? What'll you say about us ? "

" Oh, I shall say nice things about Lloyd Park

and about Hoe Street, and Essex Hall, and Highams,
and the Almshouses and——"

" Oh, yes, they're old. They always write about
old places in books, don't they ? Ain't you saying
anything about why we can't have dancing on
Sundays ? "

" I didn't know you couldn't have dancing on
Sundays."

" Well, we can't. And lots of us want it. You
say something about that in your book, and people'll
buy it. You see."

The tailor ordered three more " milky ones," one
each for us and one for the lady, who told us that
she had to get back to the shop. We finished ours
leisurely and strolled out, just as the two o'clock
result was put out on the streets. It was an unfortunate result for my companion. It seemed to
cloud the day for him ; and soon he excused himself
and said that he, too, would get back to the shop.

ILFORD

STRANDED, without company, in Waltham-stow, I sought a way out, and took a ticket on that morbid and introspective railway that passes through Walthamstow.

Do you know this secret railway? Very few people outside those who use it daily know it. Its termini are St. Pancras and East Ham. Its course describes a wiggly semi-oval, and its intermediate stations are Camden Road, Kentish Town, Highgate Road, Junction Road, Upper Holloway, Hornsey, Crouch Hill, Harringay Park, St. Ann's Road, South Tottenham, Black Horse Road, Walthamstow, Leyton, Leytonstone, Wanstead Park, and Woodgrange Park. Its scenery is varied from the sleek and respectable to the tousled, the forlorn, and the industrial. I have a terrible fancy that the people who travel along this line have never travelled any other line; that they spend their lives crawling along the northern and north-eastern edge of London. The trains are often packed; but whence the people come or whither they go, I know not. At some of the stations there is no sign of habitation or human life. Yet travellers alight at these places. Perhaps

they rest awhile in the· vasty waiting-room, or
stretch their legs along the unwieldy platform, till
the next train comes to retrieve them. They are
not as other Londoners. They have an alien, lost
air about them. One is surprised, when they speak
in the Cockney tongue; so exiled do they seem from
normal circumstances. They appear in the strange
habiliments of strange trades. One told me once
that he was a " holder-up "; another told me he
was a " clicker." Exposed laundry is one of the
principal features of the landscape. It is always
washing-day in the hamlets about this line.
Choose your time for the journey as you may,
the train will pull you through ten miles of
washing-day.

I left the train at Woodgrange Park, and walked
the gaunt length of Romford Road to Ilford. Romford Road is very long and very lackadaisical. It
seems not to want to go to Romford. I impute no
fault to it on this count ; I have been to Romford.
Somebody has crowned Ilford " the Eastern Queen."
The passion for sobriquets is often ineptly indulged.
The local guide-book says of Ilford that its population " is largely composed of City men and their
families, the husbands finding it to be a delightful
place after the rush and turmoil of the day." Perhaps: But to my mind the avenues about Lombard
Street hold peace and contemplation against the
assaulting and undelightful noise of Ilford Broadway.

Ilford offers little to the sojourner. It even taunts the eager appetite that he brings. It lacks meat; it has nothing for the voracious traveller to bite upon. Its tones are flat and wan.

After Walthamstow it comes as tepid soda-water upon an August noon. Its sorrows and its joys alike seem attenuated. It has not yet found itself. It is uncouth, leggy; plagued with the humours of the gawk. It falls between the shirt-sleevedom of Peckham and the gigmanity of Eltham; it has neither the brisk self-respect of Brixton nor the go-as-you-pleasery of Upton Park. Being so near the East End, yet of seemly aspect, it gives itself faint airs. (This magnificent mixture of metaphors pleases me.) It would like to date its correspondence from Ilford, Essex, instead of Ilford, E. Against its unpolished neighbours of the E. district—Aldgate, Barking, Stepney, Poplar, Canning Town—it is genteel. Against the wide estates of Essex it is ignoble. It is at once the patrician of the East End and the blunt democrat of Essex. It tries to look, especially at Cranbrook Park, as though it had been ravaged and brought within the borders of the East End under duress; and it does not succeed. Walthamstow is content with its lot; Ilford wears an expression of unfulfilled desire. It hungers for colour. Even the " rush and turmoil " about the Broadway have a frigid tone.

As for its neighbour, Seven Kings—well, the

guide-book tells me that Seven Kings " is an integral part of Ilford." I can well believe it.

While approaching Ilford along Romford Road—the only road in London, I believe, whose house and shop numbers go beyond 1,000—I had a feeling that I would not like Ilford. My instinct was right. I do not like Ilford. I have worked Ilford pretty thoroughly. I have " combed it out " and found nothing. Even its twelfth-century hospital chapel does not save it. This is its only architectural beauty ; and one feels that Ilford does not deserve it. More apt, more considered, is the venerable Clock Tower in the Broadway, dating back to 1881. It is imposingly placed, and one feels that it belongs to Ilford, and that Ilford is pleased with it. Two picture-palaces, in the best White City style, which first faced the " rush and turmoil " of the town ten long years ago, also belong to the family. But the twelfth-century hospital chapel seems to be a changeling.

Yet here, as at Walthamstow, the lilac was in bloom. Here were people buying beef and linen and bread. Here were trams and 'buses and Fourth " Stars " ; all the external appointments that had rejoiced me in other places. What, then, was lacking that Ilford should miss the quality of its sister suburbs ? I cannot tell. I am not good at subtleties. Make the journey, and assure yourselves. I never saw people so half-happy. The shoppers walked with pre-occupied air. Ripe appreciation of the bargain was wanting. I suppose Ilford, though forced, by economic stress, to bargaining, regards the business as a descent from its hardly-held dignity, and, like so many people, is shamefaced at doing the necessary thing, where your true aristocrat brings his native dignity to the most ignoble office. Even on Saturday nights, as I noted on later visits, the tide of human joy is at no more than half-flood. Malcontent I found on all sides ; it enveloped me. So shorn of comfort did I feel that I had to troll a stave on the spot, and could only express myself in a form as comfortless as my then state : the new *vers libre* which was invented by the Chinese some thousands of years ago :

> *At Ilford, in the early afternoon,*
> *You see very few men in the street ;*
> *But numbers of sour-faced ladies with baskets,*
> *Who exchange lugubrious gossip,*
> *And stare at the stranger with the utmost hostility ;*
> *As who should say : Where's that 'alf-brick ?*

Still, I will give it The Valentines, the most beautiful of London's natural parks. From a grapevine at The Valentines was taken the shoot that has since grown into the Great Vine at Hampton Court. The Valentines has, too, the most noble Cedar of Lebanon in London, a Tudor Lake, a Bishop's Walk, and, in the pool by its Jacob's Well, many rare water-fowl. The place itself hear-

tened me ; my warmth was increased when I discovered that there were some young people in Ilford
and that they appreciated its tranquilities. That
day they were there in groups and couples, bringing
to the bowered walks the light noise of their custom.
Whether Ilford's sweet younglings are imprisoned
during the day—only the plain ones being made
free of the streets—or whether the Valentines blesses
them all with its own beauty, I know not ; but here,
in loveliness of curl and limb and countenance, they
frolic. The boys are brave ; the girls are urgent
and bright. Ilford, though, has put its mark upon
them. Like Ilford, they are ambitious. They have
not the rough gestures of other youth. They are
grown beyond their age ; and instead of playing
vociferous games, girl looks to boy and leads him
captive. In the shy retreats they play at love ;
and when the bell is heard, warning of the closing
of the gates, you may see them coming from the
woodland, hand in hand, reluctant of the unkind
wastes of Ilford streets.

So is Ilford saved from my complete reproach.
For the sake of the children in The Valentines, one
can forgive it its Clock Tower, its corpulent municipal buildings, its bleak byways, and its hang-dog
shoppers. And that's Ilford. Having seen it, I can
better understand the case of the Silent Wife.
Twelve months in Ilford would be enough to render
the most loquacious chatterer speechless. But the

Ilford I show you here is only the Ilford that I saw. I do not forget that there must be men in distant lost places, to whom Ilford is the one corner of the earth to which at last they would come.

But its vexed laughter was too much for me. I heard the glad guffaws of other places calling, and sought my way out.   Here I suffered the last dismay. Not only does Ilford distress the stranger ; having caught him, it does its best to hold him in its chill confines.   To go to Ilford is a fool's act ; to get away from it is a knightly achievement.   It is on the edge of nothing, with a dilatory and dilapidated service to transport you to anything.   There are the foul and insanitary Great Eastern trains, which will drag you, in an hour or so, to Liverpool Street —whither nobody in his senses would want to go ; there are half-hearted tram-cars, which will carry you to Barkingside and Hainhault Forest ; there is a bald road leading to the flats of Essex ; and an unfriendly road which leads to Stratford Broadway. Choosing the least of many pains I took the road to Stratford.

Once out of Ilford, my interest revived.   A coffee-shop called " The Mitre " attracted me.   Beneath the sign was a home-made notice, the motto, per-haps, of the owner of " The Mitre," reading :

Tea Coffee Cocoa
Promptness and Sivility

I entered and called for tea, and, waiting for it, caught, from an unseen in the next pew, a human note that tickled my heart.

" Spunse cake. Last words she said to me, as I come out—don' you go'n fergit baby's spunse cake, she says. Every day she says that, though I never 'ave fergot it. No matter what state I git 'ome, I always got that spunse cake somewhere in me pocket. I wouldn't let the little —— go wivout 'is spunse cake not fer a thousand million pounds, I wouldn't."

.The tea arrived, a viscid, leathery fluid of Pussyfoot vintage, and I sipped it timorously and turned my mind from it to an *Illustrated London News* of the year before last. Then came the sensation of the day. As I gloomed over the nut-brown, through the heat and grease of the coffee-shop trickled the cool tones of a piano. This was not of itself sensational. What was sensational was that, somewhere in the upper rooms, unfeatly fingers were stumbling through the work of a modern Englishman : Joseph Holbrooke's " Ulalume." So unexpected, so incongruous was this interlude that, without intent, I ordered another cup. A Chopin nocturne in the suburbs would not have surprised me ; a Debussy fragment would not have shocked ; Chaminade, the Charles Garvice of music, one might have expected ; but to listen to an interpretation of an abstruse work by a British composer in Romford Road . . .

To that unknown musician above the coffee-shop I make this greeting. That moment was worth my travail with the dolours of Ilford. I felt as a benighted foot traveller, who amid the wet winds is suddenly warmed by the promising lights of the hospitable inn. Kind hands, that brought such unction to an Ilford-stricken traveller, my greeting !

I waited till they had rested from the keys ; then, leaving the second cup, I paid the reckoning and went. I feared that the beatitude of the moment might be broken by some drawing-room banality. I wanted Holbrooke in Romford Road as the day's nosegay.

CROUCH END

THERE is something prim and ladylike about Crouch End, that reminds one of a Mendelssohn melody. In the early coaching days, before the road to Highgate was made, it stood on the main north road, and was then a hamlet of a few poor cottages, enclosed by the country seats of the nobility and gentry. When the new road was built, it left Crouch End in seclusion; and Crouch End has grown up in tranquility, beyond contact with the gross and noisy world of traffic.

To-day, the Broadway, where six roads meet in flamboyant curves, gives an impression of busy calm. In appearance it is clean-cut and solid, and its Clock Tower does not (intentionally) offend the æsthetic sense.

"Good people" still live around Crouch End: perhaps fallen buds of the nobility and gentry of other days; and the shops play up to them, and quiet prosperity attends their endeavours. Here are shops for every shopping purpose. Their windows are opulent with the newest and the freshest; no week-before-lastism here. The assistants are alert, yet never slapdash, and the shoppers have an air of " no complaints."

In one respect it sets a noble example to other suburbs : I mean in its consideration of the wayfarer. It possesses no fewer than four restaurants, where lunch is served daily. Further, there is a baker's shop, with a full licence. Thither, at twelve o'clock, come old ladies, placid as pugs, yet with enough of vitality in them to appreciate God's gift of the grape. There they sit at little tables, with their melange of packages, and sip glasses of port or sherry, and mumble a biscuit or so.

Through the Broadway, where once stood the turnpike gate over which Ainsworth, using showman's licence, sent Dick Turpin on Black Bess, run quaint single-deck 'buses to Tottenham, Finsbury Park and Muswell Hill. So steep are the ascents, in this section of the Northern Heights, that double-deckers cannot be used. Among its other features must be mentioned the Welcome Club, conducted by the energetic Mr. Samuel Christy (not of the minstrel family) ; a pleasant road consecrated to Coleridge (Highgate, where he lived, does not even remember him) ; and the best book-shop I have ever found in a suburb. It once had a theatre called the Crouch End Opera House, but this is now a bedizened picture palace, called the Crouch End Hippodrome.

Most suburban second-hand book-shops are kept by old men with beards, and their stock is as dusty and bearded as themselves. But Crouch End's second-hand book-shop is a model of what such a shop should be. It is the property of a young man, and his stock is as spruce and youthful as himself.

You may examine his shelves for half an hour, and still have clean hands. All his volumes are what are called in the trade " bright " copies, as new. There is not one grubby item in his shop ; and his window is a delight to the eye and the mind. It makes a spot of colour in a dull road, with its gay mottoes, its mezzotints, Chinese prints and editions de luxe. Mr. Victor Whitehead is an enthusiast for the modern poets and the " younger " intellectuals, and I hope Crouch End appreciates him.

I wonder, though. For Crouch End has many tennis clubs, and when you know that a suburb supports tennis clubs, you know pretty closely its social and intellectual status. You don't find tennis clubs in Bermondsey or Hoxton, or Canning Town, or Barnsbury.

There is something about tennis that belongs to leisure and affluence. Bermondsey and Hoxton have their cricket and football clubs, for these are democratic games. But tennis is still in the swaggering stage. It is still suggestive of the pert daughter of the City man and the handsome young curate. It is still very Crouch End-y.

At Crouch End the young and the old go in for tennis. There is a nice touch of character in this.

There are people who "play" tennis and people who "go in for" tennis. The "players" of tennis are bearable; it is the others that cause the heathen to imagine a vain thing.

As in the days of the nobility and gentry there were humble cottages to set off the opulence of the dwellers on the hillside, so to-day there is a poorer quarter of Crouch End which the big Broadway has elbowed well out of sight. It hides itself modestly in Park Road, where stands the Council School; and in Park Road one finds deliberate joy in place of the kid-gloved prune-and-prism deportment of Crouch End proper.

At twelve o'clock, when school is "out," it flashes with the bright frocks and bare arms and legs of the little girls, and bubbles with the yells and warfare of the boys. At twelve o'clock, too, the "Maynard Arms" throws open its doors, and invites the traveller into its bright saloon, filled with flowers and ferns and the jovial soul of its landlord. It is a good house, with an atmosphere of quiet well-being, its walls decorated with those American "uplift" mottoes: "Work like Helen B. Merry," and so on.

Adjoining the Council School is a building that leads a double life. In the evenings it is a Gospel Hall. By day it is a restaurant, where good and cheap dinners and teas are served. It is a worthy practice, this revival of the monastic custom, and

I would like to see it adopted by all religious establishments.

It was holiday time when I was at Crouch End, and children were everywhere. In the Broadway were only the ladylike children ; but in Park Road the real children gathered to celebrate that delightful July festival—the Grotto.

Year after year this festival is kept up, with its monotonous chant of " Please remember the Grotter ! " yet not one child in a hundred knows its origin, or why it is kept in July. They have not heard of the marvellous Grotto in Spain, the resting-place of James the Less ; and how money was collected from pious pilgrims who visited it on that saint's day, each July, to keep it perpetually lighted by candles. To the children it is simply a pleasant means of making a few pence. There are many worse means.

Vulgar things like grottoes could not, of course, be allowed in the Broadway, which is so very grown-up ; but at other corners I found one-man grottoes, partnership grottoes, and syndicate grottoes. I noted one point in the management of a syndicate grotto, which showed that the ways of the City are well known to the children. The directive, business side of the concern kept well in the background, and employed a pigeon—the best-looking, best-spoken boy, with pathetic eyes—to collect the money.

I wonder, by the way, when somebody will

write a book about real children; children as
they are.

When you count the number of attempts that
have been made to interpret the child through the
medium of literature, you may say that you count
the number of failures. Never yet has the essential
child been ensnared between the covers of a book;
for how shall one seek to fasten to the printed page
an eternal, elusive miracle? Colour or line may
achieve it, but words—words may come, but they
are only words, bleak and stark and brittle. One
needs rather symbols, butterflies. It is this mystery,
this intangible something for which we have no
name, that has proved the pitfall of almost every
writer who has attempted to interpret it; for, take
up 999 books out of 1,000 in which the child appears,
and you will find that each writer subscribes to
the old nonsense that he is romantic and poetic.
He isn't. He's the most sanely materialist of all
creatures of this world. He is the apotheosis of
Common Sense, which is Genius. He doesn't believe
in fairies; he doesn't believe in anything that makes
no response to the senses; he goes one better; he
makes you believe in them. And while he builds
his dreams upon rattles, feeding-bottles, soldiers and
railway-trains—the things that men work with, and
play with, and fight with—we elders build ours upon
the transient glory with which he surrounds himself.
Try how you may, you shall never catch this glory.

In manhood and womanhood we have qualities very sharp and definite, easily distinguished, easily set down ; but to ensnare the will-o'-the-wisperie of a little girl's heart is a labour of love and tears. On canvas, of course, the thing has been done, for there is the medium through which we may approach her—colour ; and there you have her in the pictures of Murillo, Reynolds, Chabas, Ralph Peacock, and others.

Among the chief mistakes of the would-be interpreter of childhood is that of regarding the youngsters as immature men and women, which they are not. They are children—mature or immature on that plane. Manhood is a separate state of being, and has no connection with childhood, marks no stage of progression, except in so far as a piece of coal marks a progression from a bundle of leaves. I have never yet found a parent who did not regard children with a tender contempt, instead of that level, undemonstrative companionship which they all yearn for ; yet I have known little girls of twelve and thirteen who, as human creatures, were much more complete than many folk of forty. In the opposite direction, the unfortunate child is regarded as a concoction of sugar and spice. This is the safe way ; this is the way to big sales ; for nine-tenths of the public share this view—look at the success of Sir James Barrie. One can only assume that memories are very short, and that we are all inclined to look back, through a distorting glass, at those hustling, strenuous years of our childhood. How else to account for the acceptance of all the spurious stuff that is produced each year—the "Little White Birds" and the "Blue Nightingales" and the "Pink Rabbits"? There are thousands of people who, after reading such books or witnessing such plays, come away in a genuine belief that they have touched fingertips with the remote spirit of Childhood. I envy them their simple faith; and as a counter-blast to such rubbish, I should like to place in their hands a copy of Frank Wedekind's *Frühlings Erwachen*.

The lamblike love of Convention on the part of the public is proved by the fact that the three or four books which get nearest to the real child have been complete failures. The few "live" children of fiction can be numbered on the fingers of one hand. When the library reader thinks of childhood in fiction, he thinks of those detestable caricatures by Dickens—Little Nell, Tiny Tim, Paul Dombey, and the Fat Boy—and of the wistful unreality of Lord Fauntleroy or Peter and Wendy, and other creations—which too often are "made out of their own heads"—by various confectioners. Who reads Bret Harte's *Mliss* these days? Yet in Clytie and Mliss you have two human little girls, in all their unashamed naturalness, as real as any living thing. And are not Stephen Crane's Whilomville

boys the livest things in knickerbockers? Yet, who
turns to them while he may suck the syrup of Peter
Pan and Wendy and Tommy and Grizel?

And who that would not rather read *Alice* than
Les Curiosités de Lily, by Antonin Reschal? Yet
here is a man who has got nearer to the soul of the
thing than any other writer, and who, touching a
phase of child life that is for some reason entirely
glossed over by our own writers—though it is far
and away the most important phase—has pene-
trated cleanly and swiftly, as only the Latin mind
can, to the heart of the girl-child. This is a book
that should have been written many decades ago;
a book certainly that every school teacher would
do well to consider as a pendant to Frank Wedekind's terrible play mentioned above. Whoever
translates the Wedekind play into English will
almost certainly find himself in prison; yet it is
a book that should be known to all who have charge
of children; it is a gospel of childhood; it is at
once an indictment and a cry for mercy. Wedekind
and Reschal together have presented children to us
as all intelligent people know them to be. They say,
boldly and without any licentious reticence, things
that are universally known to all who have the care
of children; and things that are universally known
are invariably ignored until someone comes along
and puts them into words.

One other book I know which makes a happy

attempt at presenting the common boy: *Nash and Some Others*, by C. S. Evans, who was, for some years, a Board School teacher. In this book he has given us, for the first time, the London schoolboy as he is. One of the solemn laws of child literature is that you may only write about " nice " children. Stories about boys—even in the crude publications of Fleetway House—must be about public-school boys ; and must have for their settings disguised Etons, Harrows, and Westminsters. Little girls, in fiction, must have nurseries. On no account may you write about other kinds of children. Frankly, this seems rather rough on the twenty million other children who live in the kitchen, and learn to make love and puddings and garments before they are ten years old ; and I congratulate C. S. Evans on lifting his boot at this convention, though by doing so he has lost the popular success that might otherwise have attended his stories.

All roads from Crouch End lead uphill ; and it should therefore be a suitable spot for invalids. Indeed, there is something in its manner that suggests the valetudinarian—something subdued and heavy and contemplative. You find this " something " at Tunbridge Wells, Buxton, Harrogate, Bath, and other haunts of hypocondriacs.

A steep hill screens it from the coarse smoke of Finsbury Park, and a steeper hill shelters it from the brisk breezes of Muswell Hill. Whether its air

is salubrious or not I cannot say. It is certainly
mild and untroubled, and seems to lend its properties to the people. Maybe it's the name that
gives the place that smell of the thick warmth of
many blankets. Repeat it to yourself—Crouch End.
It is a good example of onomatopœia. One knows
what Crouch End will be like, before one sees it.

Most suburbs are happy in their names. Tooting
gives itself away in its name ; so does Bedford Park ;
and so with Palmer's Green, Catford, Barking,
Camden Town, Bayswater. Each place is so named
that the shape of the word betrays its character.
And if you say " Crouch End " to yourself many
times, you will know as much about it, as if you had
read these paragraphs.

But I am grateful to Crouch End for giving me
the adventure of the Tin Trunk. On my return
journey I took train at Crouch Hill for St. Pancras.
It chanced that it was a Saturday night of summer,
and my train was a returning Southend train, full
to its doorways. I sought the guard's van, and
fifteen other travellers made a corner for me.

Now if I have any rule of life, it is this : that if
I cannot enjoy myself, I will enjoy other people.
I had much enjoyment of other people on this
journey. A heated argument was in progress when
I entered.

A large red-faced man was holding the floor.
" I tell you I see it put out at Barking. A tin

trunk. Black. Lying over there, by you, sir. You saw that porter take it out, didn't you ? " He glared at a small man in a corner, who, thus attacked, shot nervous glances at the floor, and stammered.

" A black trunk, you said ? A tin one ? Flattish like ? I think I do remember now. At Leyton, you said ? "

" Leyton ? No ! Barking ! " barked the big man.

" Oh, I believe I see one put out at Leyton."

" Right be'ind ! " piped the guard at the door. " What's the argument ? "

" Why, that genterman over there, on the platform—'is tin trunk. Labelled for Crouch Hill, and it ain't 'ere. Taken out at Barking."

" Leyton, I think."

" Oh, well," said the guard, " he'll have to see station-master and ask him to 'phone to Barking, or wherever it was. They'll send it on."

He blew his whistle, and we steamed out. The company looked at each other and smiled and nodded. The tin trunk had broken the social ice and introduced them.

" Nice thing," said the barker. " Trunk labelled for Crouch 'Ill, and bang out it goes at Barking. I wondered why they were taking it out, but I always make it my business not to interfere. More muddling. State Control, they calls it. Baw ! "

"I don't remember seeing a tin trunk put out at Barking. I remember a bicycle going out."

"I see it, now I come to think. Oblong. Black. Lying over there."

"That's right. Not oblong, though. Not exactly. Nor yet square, neither. Curious shape. I 'ad one like it yers ago."

"Funny, but the identical same thing 'appened to a brother of mine. He was going up to Liverpool last September—no, October, I fancy. And they put his trunk out at Crewe. Only it wasn't a tin one. It was," he added, as though the difference had damped his enthusiasm for the coincidence, "it was a brown Saratoga."

"I'm positive I see it go, though I didn't notice the label."

"I did," barked the big man. "Crouch 'Ill—as plain as it could be printed. And out it goes at Barking. Only shows you how some people never use their eyes."

"Leyton, I think it was."

"I remember sitting on it when I first came in, A black trunk. Tin. Can't say I noticed the label, though."

At this point we drew into Kentish Town. A porter came to the guard, as he stepped to the platform, and held him in converse for a brief minute. He returned to his van with a sour look.

" Right be'ind ! " He turned to the big man. " Barking, you say the trunk was put out ? "

" Yes, Barking."

" No, Leyton."

" Sherlock Holmeses you are, ain't ych ? No tin trunk was put out at Barking. No tin trunk was put out at Leyton."

" But——"

" Why not ? 'Cos there wasn't no tin trunk ever put on this train. Telephone's just come through. Tin trunk's lying on the platform at Westcliff. Grr ! " .

LEWISHAM AND RUSHEY GREEN

UPON a lovely evening in September a weary pedestrian might have been seen making his way along the chalky ridge which marks the meeting of Kent and London. Undoubtedly he *was* seen, for it was a Saturday evening, and the spot was Lewisham Broadway, which, at all times loud with traffic, is, on Saturday nights, tumultuous and well-nigh impassable.

Lewisham Broadway is an affectionate little spot, and well repays any attention bestowed upon it. It stands on the Hastings Road, and is sufficiently near to Greenwich to catch a river-breeze ; and its shrubs are aided in the preservation of their hue by the water of the Ravensbourne, which flows through the Broadway. Its shops are prodigal of plate glass, and are stocked with the " latest " in everything. It has a " Boots " lending library, two or three millinery establishments conducted by " Maude," " Phoebe " and " Irene," and no visible pawnbrokers. This should give you effectually the " note " of Lewisham.

For the rest, it is a capable suburb and full of possibilities, though it has not yet developed a corporate life of its own. These little cities, like Lewisham, with their music-halls, their boulevards, their vestries, are still only a fringe of the city. I met nobody who was excited about Lewisham, as other men are excited about Guildford, or Maidstone, or Reading. Why they should not be excited, I do not know ; but if ever you see a suburban resident, suffering under the Maidstone man's praise of his Prison, or the Reading man's ecstasy about his Abbey Ruins, or the Guildford man's lyricism about the Abbot's Hospital or the Grammar School, you do not hear him respond with his Clock Tower or his Public Gardens or his new Fire Station or his old Almshouses. No ; he plays St. Paul's, the Law Courts, Kingsway, the Tower Bridge, Westminster Hall, as though he, of Lewisham or Finchley or Putney, had civic rights in them.

Lewisham's music-hall lies about a mile distant, at Rushey Green, where the shops are smaller and somewhat cheaper. The road between the two is pleasantly lined with grass-plots and enclosures of evergreens. It is a broad, brisk road, made by men who knew their job : it goes straight to the point. Rushey Green is the apex of a triangle of obscure suburbs—St. John's, Brockley, Crofton Park, Nunhead, Hither Green and Ladywell. I wonder by what abstruse system fame is accorded to suburbs ? Why is one taken and the other left ? Why are some known throughout the English-speaking world, while others, of similar characteristics, are scarcely names even to those of central London ? Why are Tooting and Surbiton known contumeliously to men in Galashiels, Cleckheaton, Runcorn Gap and Piddleford, while Crofton Park, Hatcham, Anerley, Earlsfield, Collier's Wood, remain uncelebrated ? Anerley may, perhaps, be known beyond London by the antics of one of its natives, who was celebrated in a limerick. You know it ? The one about the old fellow of Anerley, whose conduct was strange and unmannerly ? But these other places are without honour. They are not even flattered by a share of that scorn which is delivered so regularly by smart papers to Upper Tooting and Surbiton. Why they are thus ignored, I cannot say. They seem to me to possess all the best points of a truly pedigree suburb.

Rushey Green and Catford, its near neighbour, lack the bright content of Lewisham. The houses are small, and the bulk of its people leave it each morning by the early trains, after a half-masticated breakfast. There are, you may not know, three classes in every suburb, the members of which travel the same road for any distance, yet never meet. There is the class that catches the 7.30, the class that catches the 8.45, and the class that catches anything between the 10.15 and the 10.50. One feels about the people of Catford and Rushey Green that the third class is not represented among them.

They have not the air of being settled. They are only living at Catford and Rushey Green until the chance of better things presents itself.

I do not blame them. The suburbs south of the river are by no means so " desirable " as those on the Northern Heights. They are still rather more of Surrey and Kent than of London, with the worst features of both. There is no sharp dividing line between town and country, as in the North. South London, being greedy, has gobbled up territory more quickly than North London, and has not so thoroughly assimilated it. South London is a ragged back-skirt of London, trailed in the chalky dust of Kent and the brown grit of Surrey. It reminds one of the chill, bare travesty of country that one finds in Lancashire, around the mining towns.

I looked at the Lewisham Hippodrome and found it, externally, not offensive. I then inspected its bill and recognized many of the names. It has long been a standing reproach against us, among the French, that, as a nation, we take our pleasures sadly. That may or may not be true, but it is certain that we take our pleasures uncritically. So far from taking our pleasures sadly, we are most easily amused. We sit through and applaud any old thing, provided it is put over with sufficient *réclame*. We laugh loudly at, and pay big money to men who would be hissed off any Continental stage.

Visit a music-hall in cold blood, and you will agree with me. First, there is the insolence of the " house " towards its patrons. The staff keeps them waiting outside the doors until such time as they choose to open; they pack them into the cheap seats like pressed figs—" Now, close up, there ! Make room for one more, there ! Keep order there ! " —and, generally, treat them as charitable societies treat applicants for relief. Then the " bill," too, treats them in the most casual manner. Turn No. 1 on the programme is usually an " Overture," unnamed. Really, it is a military march, and the band gallops through it; and, studying the convenience of the people who really matter—the stage people—stops in the middle of the coda, and re-starts a second later with the " symphony " of turn No. 2.

The performers, throughout the evening, pay little attention to the audience. They jest with the conductor and members of the orchestra, and walk through their turns as though the whole thing were a beastly nuisance. They indulge in dialogue of a purely personal kind, and address one another by their Christian names, and make silly, obscure jokes about members of their profession, whose affairs cannot possibly interest the audience. Hardly a dozen people in any given audience follow the drift of these professional allusions; yet the whole house is kind enough to laugh—which is proof of the Englishman's traditional tenderness for the feelings of those who take liberties with him. But it is very bad for the artists. It makes them bumptious in manner and slack in work.

Sometimes the " star " turn of the bill cannot appear, and a deputy is sent on. You may have paid your money to see that one particular turn ; but try to get your money back from the box office. Recovering overpaid Income Tax from Somerset House is a facile enterprise against this.

Lingering outside the hall, in the October twilight, I heard from some dim byway, faint and sweet and far-away, that dirge of Autumn, the last of London's street cries :

> Won't you buy-uy-uy-uy
> My sweet blooming laaaaaa-
>   venderrrr ?
> There are sixteeeeeeeen
> Fine bran-shes—
>   er pen-neeeee.

It is an elegiac cry that is suited to dim suburban byways. It seems to hold in its cadences the inward yearning of all suburbs. It seemed to me, then, to express the very soul of Rushey Green. Compare it with that other cry which is still sometimes heard :

> Any ole iron ?
> Rag boddler bo !

There is heartiness in this. I don't know why empty bottles, greasy bones, cold iron, and soiled rags should inspire the wandering buyer with cheeriness ; one would rather think that the hawkers of sweet-smelling lavender should have the cheery note, and the " boddler bo " the heart-cry of the lavender man. English cussedness, I suppose.

Of the street cries that I remember hearing in my childhood, it was always the man with the unpleasant job who had the uplifting note. The dustman, grimy, with throat and nose clogged with small ash, came always to the door with a kind of " Here-we-are-again " cry of " Dust-oh ! " as who should say : " Who cares ? "   But the coalman, who was delivering goods and receiving money for them, came with a lugubrious wail of despair, rising and falling in a minor key :

" One-an-two the 'underd ! "

And the black man with the black sticks and black sack had a demoniac yell in the upper register, very fitting to his figure : " Sweeeeeep ! "

If you refer to James Hindley's book on Old London Cries, you will realize how much persuasive music has gone from the streets ; " improved " away. The street-sellers of the period with which he deals, the late eighteenth and early nineteenth century, were mostly women ; and it must have been delightful to hear their voices crying " Cherry Ripe ! " " New-born eggs—crack 'em and try 'em ! " " Fresh sweet posies ! " " Buy my brandy-balls ! " " Buy

my saveloys ! " " Dumplings, ho ! " " Colly-molly
puffs ! " " Round and sound, fivepence a pound,
scarlet strawberries ! "

I was musing thus when, so it seemed to me, I
evoked a London crier from the ground at my feet ;
for a voice close to my ear burst into song :

> Up an' down the City Road,
> In and out the Eagle,
> That's the way the money goes,
> *Pop !* goes the weasel.

" Wanter buy a stud, mate ? "

I looked round, and found the stud-merchant at
my elbow.

" Thought I'd run across you again somewhere.
'Ow y'orf fer bootlaces ? "

I bought a pair of bootlaces, and led him across
the road, his tongue pacing his feet.

" I gotter bone to pick with you, young man.
Slipping orf and leaving me like that, at Enfield.
I didn't 'arf 'ave a time."

" How ? You knew where to get the car, didn't
you ? "

" Yerce, 'tain't that. But I got in with a bunch
of nice boys, in the little place next the Church,
and I sung 'em a song or two, and they made a fair
fuss o' me, and—well, you know 'ow it is when you
get in with a nice bunch o' boys. Ten o'clock it
was when I left there—leastways, I s'pose I left—

I don't remember. I know I copped out when I got 'ome."

" Well, have you made any new songs ? I want one about Rushey Green or Lewisham."

" No, I ain't bin in no song mood lately. Roaming round the town with studs and bootlaces is all right in the summer-time, as Mark Sheridan used to say, but it's no game for this weather. Green grow the rushes-O !—don't seem to fit, does it, with October. Who wants to think of green damp things like rushes ? 'Ere—I got a new line."

He planked down his little case, and opened it, and produced a small dummy figure of Mr. Lloyd George, carried out, as the dressmakers say, in American leather. He seized this figure by the middle, and pinched it, when it shot out an impudent tongue of red rubber, upon which was printed : " A land fit for heroes."

He had given it but two pinches, when the land-lord bought one, and carried it across the bar. When I left Studdy, he had a clamouring group of ex-Service men about him, holding out their fourpences for a copy of their particular Cenotaph.

STRATFORD TO EAST HAM

I LIKE Stratford. It is joyously Cockney, while
retaining the external charms of a country
market town. It has a theatre, a music-hall,
three time-worn inns, and the Broadway, which is a
separate delight, amalgamating the charms of the
others. The Parish Church, a mere infant as a
London church—it was built in 1835—was erected as
a memorial of the Stratford martyrs who suffered
on the green in the sixteenth century. High Street,
Stratford-Langthorne, which begins at Bow Bridge
and curls round Bow Church, is a straggling lane
of tumbling cottages and over-hanging shops ; very
aromatic ; for alongside Bow Creek are chemical,
gas, oil, varnish, and pickle factories ; and the
Northern Outfall Sewer works its way here to the
river at Barking Creek.

The first Bow Bridge was erected at orders of
Matilda in the twelfth century, and remained until
1839. It was in charge of the Abbess of Barking,
upon whom fell the duty of repairing and main-
taining it. When a monastery was founded at
Stratford, the Abbess, with an air of presenting a
substantial gift, made over the bridge to the Abbot,

who got into trouble with Edward II for delegating his duties to a knave who recouped himself by demanding tolls from even the poorest passengers.

To-day, neither monastery nor nunnery may be seen ; the inns only are a souvenir of times past.

And so I came by foot to Plaistow. Plaistow seems to be full of beans. Not bands and bugles, but beans. Beans, so Eustace Miles avers, feed the brain, and the Plaistovians seem to be a brainy lot. When a Plaistovian has knocked off work, and has a quiet half-hour, he doesn't waste time at the billiards table or by picking out long losers ; he sits down and has a good read. Something light, like Kropotkin on " Fields, Factories and Workshops," Locke on the " Human Understanding," Adam Smith on the " Wealth of Nations," or Treitschke on the " Economic Determination of History." That's the kind of chap he is.

At least, I deduce that from the fact that every third or fourth building seems to be a branch of some political or municipal club, social club, organization, federation, or brotherhood. The men of Plaistow, I would say, think for themselves, and, judging from some discussions I overheard, think to some firm purpose. When a member of the courtly world, or one of their leaders of Cabinet rank, comes down to them, and tells them Thus and Thus and So and So, they want to know Why. This is most disconcerting. I do not envy the speaker who has to face them as audience. Imagine being asked, in the first stages of your preamble, when your mind is already fully distended with a flatulent address, what Karl Marx said about seasonal fluctuations ! Imagine having chunks of Adam Smith toppled into the middle of your pet anecdote about the leader of the rival party ! Even the women of Plaistow seem to know the meaning of " economics."

At East Ham the air is a little easier. Bands and bugles and recreation grounds are more popular here than beans and the economic determination of history. Of history, though, it has plenty.

Domesday Book mentions most of the parishes in this corner of the East ; and the names of vicars of the local church begin with him of 1328. That a Roman colony existed here was proved by the remains revealed by the excavations for the Outfall Sewer ; and a manor of East and West Ham was in existence long before the Normans. Its most notable relic, perhaps, is Green Street House, known as Anne Boleyn's Castle, now a school for boys.

Records do not confirm the story that it was built for her by Henry VIII, who later imprisoned her there, but it is certainly a mansion of that period, and the local authorities have so far accepted the story as to name the adjoining roads in harmony with it—Boleyn Road, Cleves Road, Parr Road, Aragon Road and Seymour Road—whose names

are five sad discords. Why Katherine Howard is
not celebrated, I do not know.

In the nomenclature of other of its streets the
Council has happily followed the custom of Paris
and perpetuated the names of famous men ; and
the random perfume of literature is wafted across
the crowded meadows of brick. Prose is celebrated
in Barking Road by Thackeray Road, Dickens Road,
Macaulay Road ; and the poets are remembered in
High Street North by Coleridge Road, Goldsmith
Avenue, Shelley Avenue, Byron Avenue, Wordsworth Avenue, Tennyson Avenue and Shakespeare
Crescent.

In Plashet, a ward of the Borough of East Ham,
lived Elizabeth Fry, the Newgate reformer, but the
house was demolished many years ago. Her memory,
however, is celebrated by Elizabeth Road, and the
tale of her labours seems to have lent inspiration to
the local Council. There is no smarter authority
than this in London. Its Town Hall strikes the
eye with an agreeable shock ; and the numerous
public libraries and branch libraries, technical college and trim parks and gardens, show that it serves
its burgesses as a Council should—namely, as keenly
as though it were a commercial enterprize out for
a profit. Even Bonny Downs, its poorest quarter,
is not so dilapidated as some parts of Bayswater
and Notting Hill.

High Street, North, its shopping centre, is a

slapdash, rakish thoroughfare, with a touch of
" I-don't-care-what-becomes-of-me " about it.   It is
never dull.   Something is always " up " in High
Street North ; a horse has fallen down, or a tram
has jolted a 'bus, or Mrs. Boffin is " putting it across "
an overcharging tradesman.   One never lacks entertainment here.   If it reflects the spirit of the East
Ham people, then they are a very jolly sort.

Indeed, they are, and they seem to know it.   One
enterprising business man has named himself Happy
Jack.   His advertisement remains in my memory :

BE A PROFITEER !

Bring your Rags, Bones, Bottles, Iron, etc., to

HAPPY JACK.

All children bringing stuff on Saturday morning have a free dip in the Silver Bran Tub.
All the kids love Happy Jack.

Other business men, not so breezy as Happy
Jack, decorate their stalls with exhortations and
appeals to the ethical sense, as : " Live and Let
Live," " We serve you as we would like to be served,"
" Our Motto is : Small profits, quick returns,"
and so on.   Mottoes seem to be generally popular
in East Ham.   In one house where I took refreshment, the walls were covered with gaily scrolled
mottoes—fifteen I counted, of which the most terse
was this : " Please don't leave your glasses on the

seat, as the practice is dangerous for your seats and my glasses."

The local guide-book comes to a conclusion with which I am in full accord—"Certainly 'dull' is the last quality one would apply to the Borough." There are residents of East Ham who speak of it as having "gone down"; who remember it—not, when it was all "vealds," but when it was a select residential suburb. Well, it may have lost some of its gigmanity, but it retains much else that is good. The houses for the most part are humble of aspect, and the shops keep in tune with them. But there is plenty of Tapley-ism about. People have work to do in these parts, and are not ashamed of being caught at it. They take the day's dish of toil with relish. With what gusto they go about it—cleaning, getting the children to school, grumbling, getting the dinner, mending, grumbling, getting the children's tea, washing-up, getting father's supper, grumbling, bathing the nippers, getting food ready for the morning, and grumbling.

Throughout the day these infelicitous streets are clattering with household tools and voices, for gossip is a great elbow-greaser; and windows and steps are cleaned, and the day's chores performed, the day's grumbles delivered, in, as the phrase goes, "no time."

There are those who, from a hurried visit, might return to speak of the afflictions of the East-

Hammers. They may save their tears and prepare to shed them about the fatigued squares of Belgravia. A longer visit would show them rich jollity, arising from hard work, enough to eat without luxury, and a little time in which to grumble over the nature of things. If they make ends meet here, they are as happy as the Chairman of a wholesale grocery company announcing to his shareholders that the profits for the past year, after deducting excess profits tax, show an increase of £40,000 over those of the past two years. And there are the Boot Club, the Clothing Club, the Christmas Goose Club, and the Slate Club ; and they get more joy from watching the amounts grow on the cards of each club than the man of means can get from an examination of his pass-book.

The bright bustle of High Street North, on Saturday evenings, is sufficient reply to those who croak of the miseries of the poor. Were these croakers permitted to bring into the lives of the poor the " simple " happiness which they so frequently expound in pamphlets, then the poor certainly would have misery enough to write home about. They don't want young University people's ideas on baby-management and house-management. They don't want their play-centres (the very Prussianism of philanthropy), their organized joy, and their mock revivals of the pleasures of three centuries gone. They want the joy of to-day, and they jolly well get it.

They don't want to be educated in the game of rejoicing. It is not an art ; it is a pastime, and anybody can play it. They don't want the thin-faced people with their Leagues of Art and Leagues of Play. Why should they allow their children to be dressed up in the costumes of three centuries past, and to be set at singing dismal songs chosen by the lantern-jawed League leaders ? It is not as though the songs chosen are beautiful songs or jolly songs. They are not, for they are chosen by the League leaders. They are chosen because they are three hundred years old. And these fatuous people want the children to dance the morris dance ; not because it is beautiful, but because it is three hundred years old. An impartial examination of the dance, and a study of old pamphlets, will show that the morris-dance is just as vulgar and immoral as jazz and the fox-trot—no more and no less.

Without doubt the hideous six-storey tenements which our cold-lipped philanthropists have thrown up here and there in our poorer districts are more hygienic and altogether better value for the wretched poor than the insanitary little houses of two or three rooms. But they are not homes. In the combat between hygiene and personal comfort, I know which side I'm on, and I know which side the wretched poor are on. A sky-line corner in a battlemented barracks is not a home. Those compact little cottages are unhealthy, you say ?

Yes, but great fun ; and, as our leading vaudeville lady has sung : " A little of what you fancy does you good ! " So long as it is what *you* fancy, and not what others think would be good for you.

East Ham has its Allotment Holders' Association, its Cage-Bird Society, its Palace of Varieties, bright picture-palaces, its High Street North, and its Mum Society. This last puzzled me when I first heard of it. I figured it as, possibly, a Quaker Society, or a Society of Codgers or some secret friendly society; I have since learnt that it is " short " for the Chrysanthemum Society.

Being within walking distance of Forest Gate, I went there to see the " Spotted Dog," for its associations with the Plague Year ; and very pleasant I found it, with its rose pergolas, bowling green and gardens. Here, from 1665-6, gathered the merchants and brokers from St. Paul's to transact their business ; the equivalent in their day of the bomb-dodgers of more recent days.

As the brokers of 1917 put the fifty miles of the Brighton Road between themselves and London, so did the brokers of those days keep six open miles between themselves and the City. Outside the " Dog " I met a celebrated local character, Sing-a-song Joe, demonstrating the origin of his name.

About him stood a cluster of youths and boys, and, when his unseemly song was done, he collected from the youths, with much badinage, a cigarette, and went happily on his way to fresh business. He is not a professional public entertainer. His method is to approach his man or youth, and ask, in the friendliest manner, for a cigarette or a share of any delicacy that the other may be carrying or consuming, promising in return—or, as some have it, threatening—to sing the benefactor a song. It is a pleasant practice, since the urban vagabond is so fast being driven from the streets. It is a return to the practice of other days, but it was not organized by the committee of any League of Arts; it is Joe's own idea.

To-day he is alone in this line; in years past he would have had to face serious rivalry. I picture the "Spotted Dog," with the mum-faced brokers gathered within, and half-a-dozen Sing-a-song Joes, slipping heads round its doors with: "How now, sirs? A merry stave or so? A catch, a glee?" followed by wrangles among the minstrels for first turn.

Master Philip Stubbes—he must have been one of those sober-side brokers—rated them soundly in a pamphlet, referring to " such drunken sockets and buffoons as range the countreyes, ryming and sing-ing of corrupt and filthic songs in taverns, ale-houses, innes, and other publique assemblies." Well, Sing-a-song Joe has the satisfaction of knowing that he is the last of a great line.

My otherwise delightful evening at East Ham

was marred by one small contretemps, for which I blame the tramways authorities. I suggest that they diversify the type in which they announce the destination of their cars. I saw a car labelled in large capitals RADOCKS. I had never heard of Radocks, and had never seen it on the map; so, filled with the lust of the explorer, I felt that I must go there, and I boarded that car. I will not record here what I said to myself when it set me down at the Royal Albert Docks.

BARKING TO CYPRUS

THE Barking Road goes to Barking and stops there, unlike the Romford Road, which continues to go to Romford after it has got there. The Barking Road goes bang into Barking, and forms the upright of a T to a cross-road. The scenery along the road is more elegiac than romantic. There are the ruins of the old windmill standing amid the marshes of Wallend; there is the sleepy river Roding; and the outlook from either side is flat, bare and bleak: void land and inhospitable distances. Here the lips of the Thames dribble into little docks and canals, whose purpose I have never discovered, for I have never yet seen them in use.

Barking itself is a medieval town, even to-day not fully modernized. It has a venerable appearance, as it should have, for here stood, in the seventh century, the richest of all Benedictine nunneries in this country. Of its old Abbey nothing was left standing, when Harry of England had done with it, save the old gateway, which still stands near the terminus of the Ealing–Barking motor-bus service. Its streets are narrow and winding and marked with poverty. It might be an old seaside town, fallen into disrepute ; an illusion occasionally heightened by a breath of Southend air brought up by the tide. Beyond it is nothing but a sorry plain of villages, mean and tawdry; for this is the London edge of Essex, whose greater part has always been forlorn of mien.

Dilapidation strikes the eye at every corner. The London edges of all home counties seem out of tune with town and with country ; but of them all Essex seems least able to pull itself together and develop self-respect. You should, however, venture into the wastes to see Eastbury Manor House, a noble Tudor mansion, that bears comparison with Hampton Court. From its sixteenth century dignity it fell to the squalid uses of a farmhouse, and was so used until a year ago. Then the National Trust stepped in and acquired it as a place of historic interest. At the time of writing the Trust is appealing for the sum of £5,000, the estimated cost of necessary repairs.

Barking gave me a bright moment. I called at a bar near the Gateway for casual refreshment, and there met the cultured barmaid. A dispute on the matter of wrong change was at its heat when I entered. The disputants were the barmaid and a slip of a fellow in Newmarket leggings.

" I know it was 'alf-a-crown,'' he was insisting. " I 'adn't got no two-shilling pieces. I shouldn't say it was if it wasn't. I ain't one of those. I

always deal fair and I expect others to deal fair.
I don't make mistakes in money. I know what
I 'ad in me pockets, don't I ? That was 'alf-a-
crown what I give yeh. I don't say you're trying
to cheat me. You thought it was a two-shilling-
piece. But it wasn't. I ain't a man to swear
black's white. I never ———''

Then came the bright moment. " Oh, shut up,"
snapped the lady. " It was two shillings. You
and your explanations ! You should remember the
old proverb : *Qui s'excuse s'accuse !* "

Geoffrey Chaucer should have heard the sharp
flick of the tongue with which the lady from Barking
gave out that *s'accuse*. She spoke it not as they
speak at Stratford-atte-Bowe. Coquelin could not
have done it better. That word from her had a
more wilting effect on the poor punter than if she
had used that English phrase to which it bears some
phonetic likeness. That, I doubt not, he could
have answered. But for *Qui s'excuse s'accuse* he
had no answer. He finished his drink and slunk
out.

From Barking I turned a little on my steps, for
I wished to finish my tramp at Woolwich, and the
only way thither was by the road that crosses the
Northern Outfall and goes through Cyprus and by
the Albert Dock. Between Beckton and Manor
Way lies lost the little colony of Cyprus. Close
here are the awesome gasworks of the Gas Light

and Coke Company. Natives will tell you that these works are kept in trim by some 3,000 toilers. This is impressive to those to whom figures convey anything. To me they convey nothing; the gas-works themselves are sufficiently exciting without a robe of figures. To see those towers and gaso-meters, as I saw them, against a cloudless twilight, is to receive a shock of wonder. Themselves hideous, they do, in that cold setting, achieve a certain gaunt and arresting beauty. To one of them Childe Roland might have come.

It is the staff of these works that mostly peoples Cyprus, though the men of Albert Dock also have made their homes in its grey streets. Who first forced by nomenclature the association with the Mediterranean Sea of this frigid, dusty region, I know not. Some sardonic wag, I guess. Here the four winds and their many branch-winds seem to meet in the leaden light of evening. It is exposed to the river, to the flats of Plumstead and to the marshes of Dagenham. At the doors of the square brick boxes that are its houses lounge or sit the men; about the stony streets the children gambol; and from slatternly windows peer the women. The men are cheerful fellows, apt and companionable. In this Cyprus they cannot live and lie reclined . . . careless of mankind. In the adjacent Albert Dock and its railway station, Gallions, work proceeds by day and night. From year to year steam-hammer,

crane, syren, hooter, bell, anvil and pick perform
their rough music ; iron against iron, steel against
steel, with a little chorus of nail and rivet ; and
through the night the shunting of trucks makes
a melancholy fugue. It is one long-drawn hysteria
of toil. Great gouts of arc-light break the body of
the dusk at a hundred points. Men come and go
in haste ; and through the stupendous clamour
tramps and destroyers crawl with an air of easy
idleness. It was once the fashion to say " Clapham
Junction " as an expression of turmoil and clangour
in the highest ; but Cyprus has outsoared the
Junction. It is one everlasting hosanna of noise,
and it is difficult to discover what it is all about.
The workmen do not try to make a noise ; they
go about their business cheerily and sedately, and
in no one corner is noise seriously created. Yet
vehement noise beats about it day and night.

But why attempt to transmit Cyprus by words?
One needs a Brobdingnagian chisel in place of pen,
a mountain of stone for paper, and an army of
jazz-band performers to work it.

Lingering about the streets I discovered that its
folk employ for their less sober conversation that
terrible medium, rhyming-slang. For this outrage
on the English language there is no justification of
any kind. The old canting tongue is a dialect,
skilfully invented ; but this farrago of sense and
sound is sheer perversion. A secret language, how-

ever complex, one can admire : it is usually cleverly made and there is a reason for it. In the crowded areas of London it is difficult for the rogue to pass information meant for a single ear, and avoid the danger of its reaching other ears. Wherefore—code language. Most of these languages derive from the Romany. Lads of the roads picked up the stuff, and it was soon passed from one to another, being changed, as it passed, to suit the occasions of those who acquired it. Then it began to pass through the usual channels of publicity—race-meetings, saloons, and music-halls, which have a much wider range than the press—so that it became twisted, until scarcely any trace of the original Romany remains. The reason for this twisting is that, as soon as a new code is formulated, it is " blown upon " by somebody, and becomes known to the enemies of those whom it was designed to protect : to policemen, narks, pawnbrokers and the public. But rhyming-slang has no such high purpose to justify its invention. It is not a secret language ; it gives itself away at once. It is a vain dislocation of current words, and its sole intention seems to be to show that the user is right up-to-date in London ways. As an example :

" Well, old pot, let's go and have a skating. I told the worry I should be water. I got plenty o' bees on me."

More esoteric and useful was the canting language

of the seventeenth century, which Dekker exposes
in his *Lanthorne and Candlelight*, thus :

" Stow you bene cove and cut benar whiddes and bing
we to Rome vile to nip a bung ; so shall we have lowre for
the bowsing ken, and when we beng back to the Dewse-a-
vile we will filch some duddes off the ruffmans or mill the
ken for a lag of duddes."

This presents little difficulty to the reader of
to-day, for, since Dekker, Henley and Farmer have
exposed the cant tongue, and there are few words
in the above whose meanings are not known. It
is worth noting, by the way, how closely Henley's
translation of Villon's ballad in slang resembles
Dekker's verse in Cant :

The Ruffin cly the nab of the Harmanbeck,
If we mawnd Pannam, lap or Ruff-peck,
Or poplars of yarum : he cuts, bing to the Ruffmans,
Or els he sweares by the Light-mans,
To put our stamps in the Harmans
The ruffin cly the ghost of the Harmanbeck,
If we heave a booth we cly the Jerke.
If we niggle, or mill a bowsing ken,
Or nip a bung that has but a win,
Or dup the giger of a gentry cove's ken,
To the quier cuffing we bing,
And then to the quier Ken, to scowre the cramp-ring,
And then to the Trin'de on the chates, in the Lightmans.
The Bube and Ruffin cly the Harmanbeck and Harmans.

Of which Dekker supplies the English of his time :

The Devill take the constable's head ;
If we beg bacon, butter-milk or bread
Or pottage, to the hedge he bids us hie,
Or swear, (by his light) i' th stocks we shall lie

The devill haunt the constable's ghost.
If we but rob a booth, we are whipped at post.
If an ale-house we rob, or be ta'en with a whore,
Or cut a purse that has a penny and no more,
Or come but stealing in at a Gentleman's door—
Unto the Justice straight we go,
Then to the Jayle to be shackled. And so
To be hanged on the gallowes i'th daytime. The pox
And the devill take the constable and his stocks.

On the philosophy of Cant he is worth hearing:

" Now as touching the dialect or phrase itself, I see not that it is grounded upon any certain rules. And no marvel if it have none, for since both the Father of this new kind of learning, and the children that study to speake it after him, have beene from the beginning and still are, the Breeders and Nourishers of a base disorder in their living and in their manners ; how is it possible they should observe any Method in their speech, and especially in such a Language as serves but only to utter discourses of villainy ? And yet (even out of all that Irregularity, unhandsomenesse and Fountaine of barbarisme) do they draw a kind of Forme , and in some words (as well simple as compounds) retaine a certaine salte tasting of some wit and Learning. As for example, they call a cloake (in the Canting tongue) a Togeman , and in Latin, Toga signifies a gowne, or an upper garment. Pannam is bread ; and Panis in Latin is likewise bread ; caesan is cheese, and is a word barbarously coyned out of the substantive Caseus which also signifies a cheese.

Within less than fourscore years (now past) not a word of this language was knowen. The first inventor of it was hang'd ; yet left he apt schollers behind him, who have reduced it into Methode which he could not so absolutely perfect as he desired. The Language therefore of canting, they study even from their infancy, that is to say from the very first houre that they take upon them the names of Kinchin coves, till they are grown Rufflers or Upright Men which are the highest in degree among them."

But of this Cyprus knows and cares nothing. For conversation on matters of no privacy at all, it is content to employ the sticky medium of rhyming-slang—with rhyme, but certainly without reason.

From Cyprus it is an easy walk to North Woolwich, where one may take the lumbering ferry to Woolwich proper. The Thames here flows with conscious pride ; and at the hour when I reached it the lights of Woolwich and of the Dockyard gave it added lustre. Great rivers, like beautiful girls, reserve their major charms for the night, and should first be seen at night. The morning character of the Thames is not without charm, but it lacks the rich hues and fluent outlines of the night. At early morning the many delicate spires of either bank toss one to the other the new sunlight, and the scum of the water glistens like hoarded wealth, and the eye receives a false effect of spaciousness, and the grimed buildings seem to be blown clean by the early wind. But in the evening the day's fair points of beauty are obscured, and new objects, unperceived by day, arrange themselves and assume the foreground of the picture. The morning has its flashes of beauty, fleeting aspects, grey cloud above red brick, brown scaffolding against torn skies, but these effects are isolated. They are, so to speak, a tuning-up for the grand symphony of the night.

Too few Londoners know their own river. You cannot scrape acquaintance with a river from its bridges and embankments ; to know it you must travel with it , and now that the Council tramboats

are no more, there is little opportunity for mingling
with the thickening life of the traffic-ridden reach
of London's river, which Zola likened to " an aquatic
Rue de Rivoli." Your only chance lies in en-
countering a friendly bargee ; and, as they say, he
wants a bit of finding. But the barge is the true
and good vehicle of river travel, its style suiting
perfectly the occasion ; and if you are so fortunate
as to secure a passage with a Jolly Young Water-
man, you will gladly forget the steam vessels and
their crowded decks.

A journey by barge from the Isle of Dogs to
Chelsea is a noble journey. At Chelsea the Thames,
as pleasure-resort, definitely ends, and thence, to
the Isle of Dogs, it is the Thames industrial. It
is this stretch of the river that is properly London's
river ; and all the varied life of the thousand acres
of the city is epitomised in these eight narrow
miles of water. Those whose humour turns to the
trivialities of travel may have beguiled themselves
at times with a mental catalogue of river-music.
All rivers have their song : some lyrical, some
jingly, some plaintive, and some swelling and sigh-
ing. There is the song of the Severn in Worcester,
so sharply marked from that of the Trent that,
by hearing alone, one could name the one from the
other. The tourist will recall, too, the slumber-song
of the Ouse at Bedford, the fretfulness of the Med-
way, the croon of the Arun, the fuss and bustle of

the Humber, and the dirge of the Exe. And all
this varied music is gathered into one stormy symphony in the Thames at London, from the mellow
grace of Chelsea to the ignoble austerities of Bugsby
Marshes.

By Chelsea, which sits in feminine repose, decked
with its rosary of great names, the river flows
serenely, as though conscious of the inspiration it
has afforded the artist. At Westminster it assumes
befitting dignity, and becomes surely the river of
a great capital : there is deep throb in its movement.
Below London Bridge the pace and volume of
sound increase, and the music of its motion is a
pompous march proper to commerce and motley
enterprise. The very hues of the water seem to
change with the changing song. From Chelsea to
Bankside it is a deep grey ; at the Tower, where
its surface is littered with a diversity of craft, it
throws up every shade of sober colour ; and below
Woolwich it settles to a harsh green. As the music
and the colour change, so does the life of its banks ;
and the river lends grace to this life, and the life
embellishes the river.

The bridges alone, seen from river level, are
a revelation to those who have seen them only
from the embankments. A stately volume might
be made on the Bridges of London—past and
present—which interrupt the curves of this section
—Chelsea, Battersea, Albert, Lambeth, Vauxhall,

Westminster, Waterloo, Blackfriars, Southwark, London Bridge (a separate volume for this) and Tower Bridge. So waywardly does the river turn and turn upon itself, that you come upon each as upon some suddenly unveiled monument.

The very names of the riverside points are an invitation to travel—Cherry Garden Pier, Cuckolds' Point, Execution Dock, Traitor's Gate, George's Stairs, Wapping Old Stairs, Horseferry Stairs, Lavender Lock, Pageant Stairs, Horselydown Stairs. How delicately they trip from the tongue! These names, though, belong to the Thames below Old Swan Pier. The solid prosperity of the stretch above that has obliterated the apt and clinging nomenclature of past times, except at Bankside, which name holds much of fragrant association—Shakespeare, Greene, Dekker, Massinger, Beaumont and Fletcher, Nash, and, much later, Johnson as auctioneer.

Between here and Lambeth one may say, roughly, that there is nothing doing. The floating fire-station, the training ship, the Thames Police-station —these are fixtures as undelightful as the Embankment hotels. Yet the two poems most closely associated in the common mind with London's river have their setting here—I mean " The Bridge of Sighs " and " London from Westminster Bridge." But neither of these, nor one of all the river poems —and how many they are—has captured and resolved its inner mystery. For the most part it is

employed as a mere framework for the human drama ;
and the poets, sheep-like, have followed one another
in finding their inspiration on the bridges and the
Victoria Embankment.

Down-stream there is always something doing.
The noise of day may somewhat abate by night,
but work proceeds.   There is a heartiness that goes
with full swing here.   The workers of this section
show a lively and sanguine disposition against the
lethargic attitudes of those whose business lies
up-stream.

There must be some subtle power, I think, work-
ing in the waters to effect this change.   If ever you
do secure a barge-trip, observe your host and his
mate, as you set out from Wapping.   Worrying their
way through the heat and stress of the traffic of
the Pool, they will be cheery of heart, with countenances of high June.   By the time the barge is
passing the Victoria Embankment, their eyes hold
the hues of mid-winter and the cheer has fled from
their hearts.   Maybe it's the loneliness of this upper
reach, maybe the unkind faces of the Embankment
buildings, the lackadaisical and voiceless work-
yards, the primness of Millbank, the sterile air that
oppress them.   Anyway, the change is wrought,
and your Jolly Young Watermen become Disgruntled
Old Taxi-men, and growl out weak curses in place
of honest invective.

Not that the barges are any sort of masters of

this art. Although the Pool is popularly regarded
as the nursery of Language, where fine young oaths
are born and bred up to be hardy maledictions,
familiar and hot in the mouth as ginger and household words, it can produce nothing in support of
that fiction. Billingsgate and Wapping live too
much, like other East End colonies, on tradition.
Doubtless the first winner of Doggett's Coat and
Badge was a fellow of fine and florid imprecation ;
but to-day the language of offence and protest lacks
variety and pungency. It is no more than a flourish
or intensive, a syncopation of an otherwise costive
phrase, signifying nothing. The three British adjec-
tives and the four foul nouns are so wearisomely
rung upon in casual conversation, that, in moments
of stress, when a suffering bargee must hold raging
and blistering language, or burst—he usually bursts.

The East End and the river are not what they
were—if they ever were. I proved this the other
day by a tour in search of our old friend, the tough.
I could not find him. Hoxton and Bermondsey
are played out ; or so it seems. I went to old-time
theatres of war, and made myself a deliberate pro-
vocation. I assumed attitudes of challenge. I
wore a ludicrous soft hat, pince-nez, brown spats,
and my usual lamb-like look. And nothing happened.

I went to Spitalfields, Stepney, Bethnal Green,
Hoxton, Haggerston, St. Luke's and Bermondsey.
In the four-ale bar of a little public-house in Spital-

fields, near Duval Street, I intentionally drank the
beer of a young gentleman of seafaring appearance ;
and he accepted my apology. Accepted my apology !
In Brick Lane I publicly contradicted a youth who
was arguing about Billy Wells. Instead of punch-
ing me on the nose for my impudence, he mildly
said that he had a right to his opinion same as what
other people had.

What can things be coming to ? One would
have thought that the turmoil of the last five years
would have left the young men of these quarters
more pugnacious, more truculent, more ready for
Mohawking than before. But no ; all is quiet.

Where are the songs of Spring Onions (that master
ballad-monger, now deceased) and the blows of
yester-year ? Where are the boys of the old brigade?
Where all the rich vagabondage, the slap-bang
nights of cakes and ale ? Standardized, I fear, out
of existence. The horrid levelling process that is
everywhere in operation is toning down high colour
and rounding the emphatic angles of character.
High spirits are frowned upon by the best young
men of these parts. Instead, they turn themselves
to the study of the form of Improbables for the
next big race, and of methods of peaceful pene-
tration. If you want to lose your gold watch, it
is waste of time to hang about Long Lane or Little
Montague Street or Bell Yard ; you will get a
quicker result in Shaftesbury Avenue or Haymarket

Fifteen years ago the costermonger passed away, and was succeeded by Bill the Basher. Now he, too, is passing. The lads of Bethnal Green and Hoxton stand about at street corners in groups more orderly than most vestry meetings. They display no sock-and-bottle activity. They have exchanged their cauliflower ears for high-brows. They no longer change hats. They no longer bash. They leave that to medical students.

I called at the Shoreditch Empire, at whose second house, in the old days, the first two turns were sure of receiving a lusty and full-throated " bird," with raspberries obbligato. Believe me, the house was as orderly as a repertory theatre ; and any turn that failed to please received no message from the audience save a bored silence.

In the public places of Haggerston and the Borough decorum and gentility prevailed. What a change from a few years back, when a famous boxer was in his hey-day. Then, public places were settings for high adventure, and the barmen kept fearful eyes on the door for the entrance of the Pedlar in full war-paint, which meant trouble pressed down and running over. But he, too, and those of his kidney, have been smothered by that blanket of propriety which step-motherly hands have put across us.

No doubt the present demeanour of the East End youth is an improvement on that of the last genera-

tion. No doubt it marks a stage of progress. And
yet . . . and yet. . . .

Thinking thus, I came to Woolwich Ferry. This
grampus of a ferry is the delight of the local children
on Saturdays and holidays. A good day on the
river may be had without expense by crossing and
re-crossing on these vessels, and the tedium of the
voyage may be relieved by games of " touch " round
the engine-house, or slides down the rails of the
gangway. My journey occupied four minutes, two
of which were occupied by a ceremonious casting
off and bringing-to. Then I was on solid ground
again, and took train from the Arsenal Station to
Charing Cross, and so home.

Printed in Great Britain by
UNWIN BROTHERS, LIMITED
WOKING AND LONDON

THE SONGBOOK OF QUONG LEE
OF LIMEHOUSE

3/6 net.　Post free **3/9**.

The Times:

A writer who knows and can give with real artistry the truth of Limehouse . . . these pieces of " Song " present the personality of Chinatown with a reality that grows more and more vivid as one reads them through.

Evening Standard:

What Thomas Burke does not know about Chinatown is not really worth knowing ; so it may be taken that Quong Lee's satiric songs fairly represent the outlook of the educated Chinaman. . . . Power and pathos are curiously blended.

Morning Post:

Mr. Burke is a prose-writer of genius, who now introduces us to a Chinese philosopher. . . . These little poems charm us so quietly that we accede to Quong Lee's request to consider them as " little cups of suey sen."

Aberdeen Journal:

Humour and a covert cynicism are found through all the poems, and there is a fragrant beauty of imagery which captivates.

Glasgow Herald:

The humourous verses are very telling, their polite detachment and frank materialism veiling their satire with an air of unconscious-ness which makes them doubly effective. . . . By the time we are finished we are more than friendly with Quong Lee.

Book Post:

Quong Lee has a very distinct personality, and it is at once pleasant and pathetic to find his arch, delicate wisdom flowering in strident Limehouse. . . . Mr. Burke is to be thanked for further enlarging our knowledge of London.

Yorkshire Observer

In Quong Lee Mr. Burke has realised a character lovable alike for its humour and its humanity.

Eastern Morning News:

Remarkable for observation and appreciation of the character of the Chinaman in London.

Ingram Content Group UK Ltd.
Milton Keynes UK
UKHW022010090323
418309UK00006B/542